Praise for *The Gentle Discipline Book*

'What I value most about Sarah Ockwell-Smith's latest book is that it honours the struggles of both children and parents. She helps us see how understanding both sets of needs yields resolution and connection, which are not words we usually associate with discipline! Readers are treated not only to fascinating new discoveries about how children's brains and behaviour relate but also to the "ah-ha" moments that parents most wish for during times of conflict with their children.'

Dr Suzanne Zeedyk, Developmental Psychologist,
Honorary Fellow, University of Dundee

'In *The Gentle Discipline Book*, Sarah Ockwell-Smith challenges us as parents to pause, take a step back and understand why children behave the way they do, so that we can make respectful and effective parenting choices. Our society tends to view gentle discipline as taking a passive approach but Sarah explains clearly, using science-backed examples, why that simply isn't the case – gentle discipline is the kind and logical way to guide our children as they develop and change emotionally and mentally. And it prevents us from turning our homes into battlegrounds.

The guidance is applicable for parents with children of all ages, and Sarah eloquently takes a complex subject and makes it accessible and easily understood. Her no-nonsense yet gentle approach is refreshing and empowering to parents, encouraging us to view our children as individuals and to be responsive to their needs, rather than applying a one-size-fits-all approach to discipline. Sarah also tackles related issues, such as dealing with

criticism from friends and family, and offers real-life wisdom on how to deal with judgement, whether real or perceived. She also dedicates a chapter to parents, highlighting why dealing with our own demons – and the subconscious triggers we all have – is one of the most important aspects of charting our parenting course. Congratulations Sarah, this is a comprehensive, pragmatic and common-sense approach to redefining what it means to discipline our children. Children all over the world will be thanking you!'

Tracy Gillett, writer, mother and
founder of *Raised Good*

'As a sleep-deprived first-time mum, surrounded by a pile of books that were in complete conflict with my parenting instincts, my life was changed when I discovered Sarah's gentle sleep techniques and advice.

Fast forward almost two years and I am now the mum of a wonderful sleeper, but find myself presented with a whole new world of confusing information about discipline. Once again the 'traditional' messages of discipline in our society go against how my husband and I want to raise our family, so reading *The Gentle Discipline Book* has been a wonderful eye-opener for me. I now know how my child's brain and emotions are developing, allowing me a greater understanding of *why* he does things and, more importantly, why he will do things in the future as he develops.

Sarah's advice has given me the confidence to know there are alternative, gentler methods to things like the naughty step, and I'll be using this book as my bible for the next 16 years! And recommending it to *all* my friends.'

Charlie O'Brien, presenter, blogger,
vlogger and mum to Noah

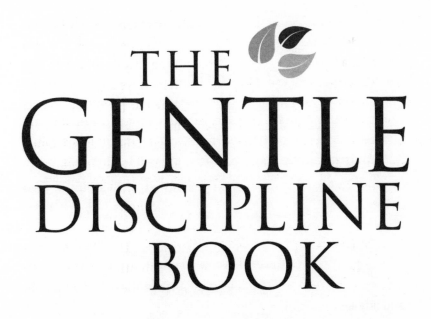

THE GENTLE DISCIPLINE BOOK

How to raise co-operative, polite and helpful children

SARAH OCKWELL-SMITH

piatkus

PIATKUS

First published in Great Britain in 2017 by Piatkus

7 9 10 8 6

Copyright © Sarah Ockwell-Smith 2017

A CIP catalogue record for this book
is available from the British Library.

ISBN 978-0-349-41241-2

Typeset in Stone Serif by M Rules
Printed and bound in Great Britain by
Clays Ltd, Elcograf S.p.A

Papers used by Piatkus are from well-managed forests
and other responsible sources.

Piatkus
An imprint of
Little, Brown Book Group
Carmelite House
50 Victoria Embankment
London EC4Y 0DZ

An Hachette UK Company
www.hachette.co.uk

www.improvementzone.co.uk

About the author

Sarah Ockwell-Smith is the mother of four children. She has a BSc in Psychology and worked for several years in Pharmaceutical Research and Development. Following the birth of her first child, Sarah re-trained as an Antenatal Teacher and Birth and Postnatal Doula. She has also undertaken training in Hypnotherapy and Psychotherapy and is a member of the British Sleep Society. Sarah specialises in gentle parenting methods and is co-founder of the GentleParenting website (www.gentleparenting.co.uk). She also writes a parenting blog (www.sarahockwell-smith.com). Sarah is the author of five other parenting books: *BabyCalm, ToddlerCalm, The Gentle Sleep Book, The Gentle Parenting Book* and *Why Your Baby's Sleep Matters*. She frequently writes for magazines and newspapers, and is often called upon as a parenting expert for national television and radio.

Contents

Acknowledgements

I would like to say a big thank you to the parents who allowed me to publish their questions and comments in this book and also to those who answered my many questions about what to include. I hope I have written the book that you all asked for.

As ever I am indebted to my children for teaching and showing me what I am doing wrong as a parent, as well as, sometimes, what I'm doing right. I hope that as we move through our journey together you will consider that I have done more 'right' than 'wrong'!

Lastly, thank you to you, the reader, for choosing to read my book. I hope you enjoy it.

How to use this book

I deally, you will read this book in its entirety for the best results and most comprehensive understanding. If, however, you are desperate for a specific 'fix', I would recommend that you start by reading Chapters 1, 2 and 3 and then skip to the chapter relating to your particular concern. Some of the scenarios in the book relate to certain ages; however, the theories underpinning my suggestions are universal and, as such, can be applied to children of any age. In fact, a lot of them can be used to help your relationships with other adults too.

Lastly, no matter what your concern, Chapter 14 applies to everybody. If you don't discipline consciously, your efforts will probably be far less effective. So, even if you think Chapter 14 isn't for you, I would strongly recommend that you read it. In fact, the more irrelevant you think it is to you, the more likely it is that you need to read it!

Introduction

would like to begin by letting you in on two secrets. The first is that children probably wish that they didn't misbehave just as much as parents do. The second is that almost everything we think we know about disciplining children today is wrong.

As a parent of four, I can understand how hard it is to always work *with* your children, especially when they are pushing your buttons. And most of us don't have the luxury of focusing solely on parenting: there are bills to be paid, jobs to be done, elderly relatives to be cared for. We have to balance so much, often more than is possible for one person. So it can be easy to slip into old patterns of shouting and punishing – perhaps a subconscious throwback to our own upbringing. The key to good discipline, however, lies in our behaviour and actions, and throughout this book we will consider how much our feelings and, indeed, self-discipline matter. A scary thought indeed. I'm not saying you need to be perfect. Far from it. I have made many mistakes as a parent; I still do. And mistakes are OK, so long as you learn from them. Really, this is what good discipline is about: learning – about your child and yourself.

My goals with this book are to help you to understand why children misbehave and how to respond in a way that is both effective and gentle. Many of society's most common discipline methods today cannot claim to be either. Current understanding of discipline is steeped in old behaviourist understandings – the belief that children need to be punished and motivated to do better. The reality is that while discipline that focuses on punishment and motivation may appear to produce quick results, the long-term effects can leave parents with a far worse problem than they had initially.

Many people ask whether not punishing at all means that you mollycoddle your children and let them walk all over you? This is my top bugbear! Our society is entrenched in an authoritarian style of parenting and the idea that if children are not punished for their misdemeanours, they will rule the roost and become unruly and disrespectful. The true key to better behaviour though is in working with, not against, your child. View yourselves as a team, rather than two enemies battling against each other to see who can 'win'.

Understanding *why* and *how* children behave should come right at the very start of any book about parenting and discipline. For this reason, the first three chapters of this book look at the science of behaviour and learning. Once we understand why children behave in a certain way and what makes them learn, we very quickly realise that most common discipline methods in society today are wide of the mark and often completely fall short of their claims. In many cases, 'bad' behaviour is not the child being deliberately defiant, but an indication that the behaviour expected of them is at odds with what they are capable of doing and feeling at any given moment in time. If anything is to blame, it is our unrealistic expectations and demands.

What of modern-day discipline methods that focus on motivating children to do better – a method commonly employed in day care and schools? Their one big failing is that they presume the child *can* actually do better. But what if they can't? What if they lack the necessary ability and development? These motivational tools will only work if the child has the requisite skills to turn things around. And in many cases they simply don't. So the child is effectively being punished for not being able to do better. Imagine the effect this has upon their self-esteem. This is important for all who have – or who work with – children to understand, as a lack of self-esteem is often at the root of many behavioural problems (this is discussed in depth in Chapter 13). Could the prevailing approach in most education settings therefore be making the behaviour of many children worse? Chapter 5 looks at current discipline methods in education and childcare today, before moving on to discuss why the most prevalent approaches are wrong and, perhaps most importantly, what parents can do to make things better and undo any negative effect.

In Chapters 6 to 13 we will look at the specifics of discipline. Many parents struggle when it comes to choosing which method to use with their child at any time. These chapters will make things a little easier, as I introduce you to my idea of 'Why? How? What?' This is a very simple way to make sure you use the best discipline method possible, based on consideration of *why* your child is behaving in the way that they are, *how* they might be feeling and *what* you hope to gain from disciplining them – something that we will keep in mind throughout these chapters.

As well as providing you with a framework that will enable you to become the expert in your own child's behaviour and discipline, I have included some solutions to particular issues. These will help to get you started until you are confident with the methodology and its application. I have also included question-and-answer sections at the end of each of the specific behaviour chapters. The questions (from real parents) and their answers focus on gentle-discipline solutions and, alongside my empowering framework, will allow you to get the most from this book and understand how to apply the techniques to your own children.

What is discipline?

Over the last few years I have asked many parents this question. Common answers include:

- setting boundaries

- guiding children

- behaviour management

- teaching right from wrong

- teaching social rules and expectations

- helping children to fit into society

- keeping children safe

- children understanding consequences

- making children into nice people

- raising respectful children

- teaching children self-control

- enforcing limits

- instructing children to be 'good'.

The *Oxford English Dictionary* defines discipline as: 'The practice of training people to obey rules or a code of behaviour, using punishment to correct disobedience.' This fits the idea of discipline most commonly used in society today, where it is all about punishment and viewing the child as naughty. It wasn't always this way though; there was once another definition – one that focused on teaching and learning. The word discipline is based on the Latin word *disciplina*, which means 'instruction'. *Disciplina*, in turn, derives from the Latin *discere*, which means 'to learn'. *Discipulus*, which gives us the word 'disciple', also derives from the same word, and denotes a pupil. Perhaps the most famous disciples were the students of Jesus, which, by extension, makes Jesus the teacher. I think most would agree that Jesus is portrayed as gentle in almost all Bible stories.

What is gentle discipline?

Gentle discipline is focused upon teaching and learning, rather than punishing, and having expectations for children's behaviour that are realistic, given their level of brain development. It is also about mutual respect and working *with* children, not against them. In gentle discipline there is a balance of power; it is not held solely by parents. It is about having humility and patience, being mindful of your own triggers and demons as a parent and not subconsciously projecting your issues onto your child. It is about setting boundaries and limits and enforcing them with compassion and respect. Gentle discipline is about positivity and planning for the future. It is about inspiring children to be better and do better, while you work to set a great example to them.

What is gentle discipline *not*? It is not permissive; it isn't a pushover. It is not about letting your children get away with everything and raising self-entitled, disrespectful brats. It is certainly not lazy or accidental. While a lot of people know what authori*tarian* and permissive parenting are, few know the real meaning of authori*tative* parenting – the position that gentle discipline takes.

Authoritarian

Authoritarian discipline styles have incredibly high expectations of children's behaviour – often a lot more than they are capable of. They demand that children 'should be seen and not heard' – that they should effectively behave in the same way as adults. They leave little room for compassion, empathy or understanding, labelling children as 'naughty' and focusing on teaching a lesson. The parent has full control and the child has none. The most common discipline methods today are authoritarian and include time out, the naughty step, grounding, smacking/spanking, shaming, detention and exclusions, sending the child to their bedroom and taking away their possessions.

Permissive

Permissive discipline is a misnomer, because permissive parents rarely discipline. This is the style that lets children 'get away with it'. Expectations of behaviour are often too low. Permissive parents often say, 'Ah, he can't help it, he's only little', when excusing a behaviour that actually is not age-appropriate. Boundaries are rarely enforced – if they exist at all. This is often due to the parent being too scared of making the child cry because they feel so compassionate towards them that they never want them to be upset.

Authoritative

Authoritative discipline methods walk a careful line between parental and child control. When it is appropriate, the child is given control; when it is not, the adult takes the reins. Expectations of behaviour are realistic: not too much and not too little. Discipline is always conducted with respect and compassion. Parents are not afraid of their child crying, but when they do cry, often as a result of discipline, they are supported and offered comfort.

This book focuses on authoritative discipline methods, or as I like to call it: gentle discipline.

Becoming a great teacher

Think back to when you were at school. Did you have a favourite teacher – somebody who inspired and motivated you? Perhaps someone you really looked up to? If you could describe their personality, what traits would you say they had? I'll bet they were, among other things:

- inspiring
- a good role model
- patient
- reliable
- diplomatic
- knowledgeable
- understanding
- optimistic
- fair
- caring
- creative
- funny

- approachable

- humble

- always learning/keeping up to date with their subject

- easy to talk to

- respectful

- adaptable

- broad-minded

- firm

- kind.

In fact, if you were to write a job description for the perfect teacher, you would probably include many of these traits.

Over the next three chapters we will look at ways in which you can hone your innate teaching skills to best discipline your child. A great teacher is one who stays calm, controls their temper and inspires their students by setting a great example; similarly, the most important thing you could ever do as a parent is to exorcise your own childhood demons, remove or reduce triggers and learn how to rein yourself in. All of this is covered in some detail in Chapter 14.

And don't be afraid to question when discipline is truly necessary. Very often we feel obliged to discipline, not because of a conscious decision we have made, but because we sub-consciously feel we should. Throughout our lives we pick up on the expectations of others, whether we agree with them or not, and no expectations are more powerful than those of our own parents and teachers. Gentle discipline is about becoming conscious. It is about breaking the cycle of repeating what has gone before, just because that's the way it has always been. It is pioneering and paradigm shifting.

What makes a good student?

Now think about a good student you knew at school. Somebody who always tried their hardest. What traits did they have? Were they:

- motivated
- focused
- ambitious
- tenacious
- resilient
- optimistic
- brave
- eager to learn
- hard-working
- inquisitive
- a free thinker
- confident
- resourceful
- proactive
- determined
- persistent
- independent?

Ironically, many of the things that we find so difficult to handle in our children – behaviours deemed 'naughty' and undesirable by society – are rooted in traits that they need to be good learners and reach their full potential. Let's look at the list again and see how some of these can be viewed in a different light:

- Motivated, ambitious, determined and tenacious: a child with these qualities can also often be called 'stubborn'.

- Focused: this can translate into a child who 'doesn't listen' (if you ask them to do something when they are engaged in another activity).

- Resilient: a child who 'doesn't learn from punishment'.

- Brave: a brave child might be considered 'disrespectful'.

- Eager to learn: a child who touches everything.

- Inquisitive: can be thought of as constantly asking annoying questions.

- A free thinker: a child who 'backchats' or asks, 'Why should I?'

- Resourceful: a child who gets 'into everything'.

Reframing your view of your child's behaviour can help both you and them; by understanding and accepting that some of the things you struggle with now can turn into wonderful traits when they are older, you can make your relationship with them much easier.

It isn't just children who are students, or learners. You are too. The best teachers never stop learning; and the same is true of parenting. There are no perfect parents, or ones with all of the answers. We are all learning, all the time. Good discipline is about flexibility and humility. The teacher/student roles swap every day, often every hour – particularly when our children are teaching us something important. Sometimes, they may even teach us that the way we are disciplining them is not working, and as parents, our role is to learn from that and adapt. As Walter Barbee, President Emeritus of the Family Foundation of Virginia said:

> If you have told a child a thousand times and he still does not understand, then it is not the child who is the slow learner.

There is a big difference between disciplining in the short term, to make life easier as a parent, and disciplining to 'grow' your child into the person you would like them to be in the future. The most common discipline methods today are very much focused on the short term. A more effective – and, indeed, positive – approach considers the future as well as the present.

Gentle discipline in practice

You have free will. At any moment you can step away from the well-trodden authoritarian path and walk towards creating a better future for your child. But how? It starts with making a space between your child's behaviour and your resulting discipline. This space affords you time to think about what you're doing and whether your actions will meet your long-term parenting goals. Too many parents discipline in an angry, reactive way. If you do this, you will always fall into an authoritarian style, or that of a poor teacher.

Before you discipline, you should always pause and ask yourself, 'Why do I feel the need to discipline my child?' If the answer is anything other than, 'Because I would like my child to learn that what they have just done is not appropriate, or there is a better way to do it', then you should not discipline. It doesn't matter how many people are looking at you or what the voice inside your head from your own childhood is saying ('You would have got a smack or been sent to your room if you'd done that'). Gentle discipline is about conscious, mindful decisions. Whatever situation you find yourself in it is imperative that your actions are performed mindfully. And to be mindful you have to stop and become aware. This is what I mean when I talk about putting a space between your child's behaviour and your response. It is fundamental to gentle discipline and, as such, it underpins the whole principle.

SPACE denotes five steps towards effective, gentle discipline:

- **Stay calm**

- **Proper expectations**

- **Affinity with your child**

- **Connect and contain emotions**

- **Explain and set a good example**

Stay calm

When your child presses your buttons and you feel yourself getting stressed or angry you should absolutely not discipline them until you are calm. Take a deep breath, hold it for a few seconds and slowly exhale. Repeat as often as necessary until you can think more clearly. Sometimes, you may have to give yourself time out. That is, move away from your child temporarily, so that you can think more clearly.

Proper expectations

You wouldn't punish a fish for not being able to walk or a cat for not being able to talk. Yet many authoritarian discipline methods punish children simply for being children, with their age-appropriate level of brain development. Before you respond to your child's actions ask yourself, 'Do they understand what they have done? Could they control it? Do they have the brain development to do better?' If the answer is 'No', your response is likely to be very different. (Chapter 3 discusses what children are – and are not – capable of at any given age.)

Affinity with your child

Gentle discipline requires you to separate your dislike of your child's behaviour from your feelings towards them. Too many parents mix up the behaviour and the child. Your child remains the same one that you love dearly, no matter what they have done. Having an affinity with somebody means that you have a connection and an understanding of each other. It is this understanding, this empathy, that will aid you in disciplining your child gently. Hold on to it, whatever your child has done. Remind yourself of how much you love them and try to view their actions from their perspective. Ask yourself why they did what they did? And how are they feeling? This will not only help you to understand their actions, but also to solve the problem and discipline appropriately, as well as to stay calm.

Connect and contain emotions

Earlier on I let you in on two secrets. The first was that children would probably prefer that they didn't misbehave just as much as parents do. This is so true. In Chapter 1 we will look at the most common reasons why children misbehave, and in Chapter 3 we will consider what their brains are capable of doing at any given age. At all ages, however, children need their parents to guide them and help them to manage their feelings. We have a level of brain development that they just don't have, even as teenagers. We are mature enough to 'hold' some of our child's big feelings as well as our own, to help them to calm down. Of course, in order to do this, we have to look after ourselves too. The secret to emotional intelligence is knowing that all emotions are OK; it is how we manage them that matters. Until your child learns how to manage their emotions, it is your role to externally manage them, while leading them in the direction of self-control. To contain your child's feelings, you must connect with them. Your compassion and support will guide them towards becoming the person you hope they will be. The best discipline happens when you work as a team.

Explain and set a good example

This stage can only happen when both you and your child are calm and well connected. One of the main reasons why discipline fails is because of a lack of one of these, or sometimes both.

Explaining should be age-appropriate. Your communication with your child needs to be at a level that they understand, and often discipline falls short here too. Think carefully about how you will communicate. It isn't just your words that matter, but how you say them too. Your child is watching you just as much as they are listening to you. If you shout, you indicate to them that not only is shouting OK, but it's what they should do when they are angry with somebody or when somebody does something that they do not like. If your child hits somebody, the very last thing you should do is hit them in the name of discipline. If you do, your example shows them that hitting is OK, and that it's a desirable way to resolve differences and conflict. Your explanation and example should show your child, clearly, how to handle situations. After all, as we've said, the best teachers lead by example. The same is true for discipline.

Putting SPACE between your child's actions and your discipline allows you to focus on your true goal – that of teaching your child to do and be better. Of course, your teachings need to be flexible. All children are unique and all situations, even with the same child, are unique. Working with SPACE should hopefully put you on the right track though. In Chapters 6 to 13 I will cover many different examples and specific situations, all keeping SPACE in mind. If your specific concern is not included, work through each point carefully and you will almost always reach an effective and gentle-discipline solution.

When should discipline start?

Many believe that discipline is something that should be introduced during the toddler years, but that babyhood should be 'discipline free'. All parents, however, begin to discipline their children from the time they are born. Discipline is simply teaching and learning. From the moment you hold your baby in your arms you are teaching him, just as he teaches you. If you hold him in a certain way and he cries, you quickly learn to change positions. You speak to him and he babbles back. This is discipline.

Should discipline change as your child gets older? Surely you don't discipline a teenager in the same way as you would a toddler? Actually, the basics remain. Your expectations of the developmental capabilities will change with age, but your underlying approach should stay the same: a position of understanding, respect and empathy.

You are the best teacher that your child will ever have. Yours is the greatest influence of all. Every minute of every day you are disciplining your child; you may not be aware of it, but you are. Little eyes are always watching you and ears are listening to you. But whatever age your child may be, however you may have previously disciplined, you can always change. It is never too late. Gentle discipline works for everybody, regardless of how long it has been practised, because it is based on the unique needs of each individual child.

So how do you do it? Read on!

Chapter 1

Why Children Misbehave

In this chapter we will look at the most common reasons for misbehaviour – that is children's behaviour that is deemed undesirable and difficult. It is impossible to discipline gently and effectively without a good understanding of the triggers of misbehaviour. Far too many experts concentrate on 'fixing the problem' without helping the parents to understand why it happened in the first place. Any discipline that focuses solely on 'the solution' actually disempowers you as a parent. Remember that a good teacher has a good understanding of their subject, and to achieve this they must first take the place of the student. Understanding the reasons for your child's undesirable behaviour is the starting point for knowing how to improve it. So with our student hats on, let's step into the world of the child and try to understand things from their point of view.

Do you ever tantrum? As adults we tend to refer to our own tantrums as 'losing control', 'exploding' or 'meltdowns'. Similar words are used to describe tantrums in the teenage years. The fact is that everybody, regardless of age, has to deal with overwhelming emotions at some point, and some cope with this better than others. In fact, we often expect behaviour of our children that we are not fully capable of ourselves.

Life is difficult and confusing. We all have a lot to deal with on a daily basis, and if we as adults don't navigate the journey perfectly at all times, then we have no right to demand that our children do. So accepting that your child will have meltdowns and tantrums, just as you do sometimes, is perhaps the best way forward. Resetting your expectations, starting with the baseline that everybody misbehaves, is a great starting point. Next comes an understanding of why we all misbehave. The discipline only comes in after this – when you aim to calm the misbehaviour. Too many people jump straight in at the 'fixing' stage without giving any thought to the whys and wherefores.

In Chapter 3 we will look at the neurological basis of behaviour and how this changes during childhood. The human brain differs dramatically from babies to teens to adults, which means it is unrealistic to expect children to behave in the same manner as adults. Perhaps the largest difference is in the area responsible for impulse control and regulation of emotions – which is why resetting expectations for behaviour, so that they are age-appropriate, is so fundamental to gentle discipline. For the remainder of this chapter, however, we will focus on non-neurological causes of undesirable behaviour, although the two are always linked. There are undoubtedly environmental triggers, but a child's brain – whether they are a teen or a toddler – is not like that of an adult, and this immaturity will always play a role in their undesirable behaviour, simply because they cannot control their actions as well as an adult can.

Physiological behaviour triggers

Have you observed that particular triggers of your child's behaviour are of a physiological nature? My children are all noticeably more cranky when they are tired, hungry or when they have had too much screen time. I can also tell when they have had friendship issues or trouble at school by their behaviour. Knowing their triggers allows me to prepare for, pre-empt and – sometimes – avoid any related bad behaviour. It also helps me not to take their behaviour personally. From the child's point of view, it's useful if they can recognise and avoid triggers independently, without parental help, although it is the parents' role to teach them about these initially. While toddlers, pre-schoolers and even infant-school children might understand the negative effects of certain behaviours, it is quite unlikely that they will always be able to avoid them without parental help. But in the tween (roughly ages eight to thirteen) and teen years children can become quite proficient at avoiding certain triggers without any adult input.

So let's explore some common behaviour triggers in children of all ages. They are in no particular order, and the list is by no means complete. Remember that each child is unique and triggers reflect this; finding your child's own triggers is most important.

Diet

For many children, diet can play a tremendous role in their behaviour, and parents often notice significant changes after focusing on this for several weeks. Despite popular opinion, sugar does not make children hyperactive. It is undoubtedly not healthy, but poor behaviour is frequently wrongly blamed on a 'sugar rush'. Conversely, low blood sugar, or, rather, low blood-glucose levels, may affect behaviour. The body releases a compensatory amount of adrenaline in response to a fall in blood glucose, known as hypoglycaemia. This chain of events can cause a negative change in behaviour – a phenomenon sometimes referred to as being 'hangry', a combination of hunger and anger, largely caused by the change in glucose and adrenaline levels. Making sure that children avoid becoming overly hungry may have a positive effect on behaviour.

One thing that does certainly have an effect on behaviour is artificial additives or E-numbers. In 2007, a study found that the consumption of food containing any of the following six additives in particular significantly increased hyperactive behaviour in children between the ages of three and nine[1]:

- Sunset yellow (E110)

- Quinoline yellow (E104)

- Carmoisine (E122)

- Allura red (E129)

- Tartrazine (E102)

- Ponceau 4R (E124)

Common sources of E-numbers that may cause hyperactivity in children include breakfast cereals, crisps, sweets, fish fingers, juices and children's medicines. If you think that your child may be affected, be sure to check the ingredients' lists on product packaging.

But it's not just additives that can negatively impact behaviour. Deficiencies in children's diet can also play a part. In 2013, research on almost five hundred children aged between seven and nine years found that low levels of omega-3, long-chain polyunsaturated fats (LC-PUFA) were associated with increased behaviour problems, a lowered reading ability and poorer memory.[2]

If you suspect that your child's behaviour may be worsened by dietary triggers, the place to start is with a food diary, noting everything your child eats and their behaviour daily over a couple of weeks. This can help to provide insight into any negative reaction to foodstuffs, particularly E-numbers. Analysing their diet can also help to highlight any nutritional deficiencies. Ideally, all of your child's nutritional needs will be met via their diet. LC-PUFAs for instance can be found in oily fish, such as mackerel, salmon and tuna, as well as flaxseeds, which can be easily added to breakfast cereals. Many nutritionists suggest that if a child's diet is low in LC-PUFAs they would benefit from omega-3 supplements, particularly if they are prone to hyperactive behaviour.

Lack of sleep

Have you noticed a change in your child's behaviour when they are tired? Toddlers who have skipped a nap tend to be grouchy, short-tempered and sometimes clumsy. The same is true at any age. I can always tell when my teenager has had a late night for exactly the same reasons.

But how long should your child sleep for? Nobody really knows. At best, experts can provide fairly broad ranges for each age; however, sleep needs are unique and while some children survive perfectly well on eight hours' sleep in a twenty-four-hour period, others may need nearer to twelve. The table below, based on advice from The National Sleep Foundation in the United States of America, is a good guide to sleep needs by age:

Age	Average sleep need per twenty-four-hour period
1–2	11–14 hours
3–5	10–13 hours
6–13	9–11 hours
14–17	8–10 hours

Bedtimes that are too early, as well as too late, can mean that a child will not get enough sleep. If they are put to bed before their body is biologically ready for sleep, research shows that they take longer to get to sleep and are more likely to wake overnight.[3] A good bedtime for children under eleven years of age is somewhere between eight and nine o'clock. Teenagers, on the other hand, are not biologically ready for sleep until much later. Research shows that the sleep patterns of thirteen- and fourteen-year-olds undergo a phase delay, a tendency towards sleeping at later times.[4] This applies to both bedtime and wake time, with a typical sleep onset time of eleven o'clock at night. The problem here is that at this age most children still need at least eight or nine hours' sleep per night, yet they are expected to get up for school. The early school start is at odds with their biological sleep needs, which invariably means that they go to school having had too little sleep – and this sleep deficit can create many behavioural problems.

In addition to bedtimes, the other major issue children struggle with when trying to get enough sleep is lighting. Research has shown that blue, or short-wave, light sources trick the brain into thinking it is still daytime and inhibit the body's secretion of the sleep hormone melatonin.[5] Any night lights in your child's room that are not red (in terms of the light emitted) can inhibit their sleep. Red light is the only one that does not inhibit the secretion of melatonin. And it's not just conventional lighting that causes an issue with sleep – screens such as televisions, smartphones and tablets also emit large amounts of blue light. So these devices keep children awake due to biological responses, as well as the obvious temptation to play on them. Screens have no place in your child's bedroom, or even in the hour or two leading up to bedtime.

Environmental overwhelm

Have you ever felt truly overwhelmed by your environment? Perhaps a place filled with many different smells, loud sounds and lots of people bumping into you? I personally find the London Underground to be a bit of an assault on my senses and whenever I travel into London I am always grumpy and exhausted for the remainder of the day.

Many years ago I was exhibiting at a baby show in a very large hall which was lit by rows of spotlight tracks suspended from the ceiling, bathing everything in high levels of artificial light. My stall was located next to the stage where several product demonstrations and fashion shows took place throughout the day, all accompanied by loud music, while the smells of toiletries, aromatherapy and curry, from a nearby food stall, filled the air. At least a thousand people attended, jostling each other and navigating prams and bug-gies through the busier areas. At the end of each day's exhibiting I went home with a pounding headache due to the sensory overload, while almost all of the visitors at my stall complained that their children were grumpy, grizzly and irritable, although most greeted me with, 'Hi, I'm sorry, I don't know why my child is so unhappy.' I told them all to look up at the bright lights and imagine how they would feel if they were reclining in a pram or a buggy and staring at them throughout their visit. Then I asked them to imagine being surrounded by hundreds of pairs of legs bumping into them and trying to sleep through the throbbing music and the cries of other children in their ears. And then I asked if they would feel irritable in the same situation. Sometimes, stepping into the shoes of your child can give you all the answers you need.

Now imagine how your child feels when they start school for the first time at the age of four or five. At nursery or preschool they were used to a small space and probably fewer children. Once they start school they are, for one thing, the youngest, usually out of at least a hundred children. The buildings are bigger and the sounds amplified. Is it any wonder they struggle with feelings of being totally overwhelmed? Imagine also going through all of this again at the age of eleven. Starting secondary school is by far the most difficult transition for most children. If you found yourself in a new environment and battling to make sense of it all, you might find that you were grumpy and short-tempered at the end of the day too. And imagine that you've been trying hard to 'keep it together' all day, but that now you're home, with those you love and trust, you can finally 'let it all out' and release your authentic emotions. So many children go through this when they start a new school, yet their parents don't understand why they are irritable and 'naughty' when they get home. They complain of school reports that speak of a child who's polite and mature, yet at home they are anything but. This behaviour is so normal – the child is finally home from nursery or school and feels it is safe to drop the façade in the presence of people they love and trust. For parents this can be hard to handle, especially if they believe that the child is being 'naughty on purpose'. In fact, their behaviour shows what a great job the parents are doing, by making their child feel secure and supported enough to be able to show their true emotions.

Although most children will battle with feelings of being overwhelmed at specific points, there are others who struggle a lot on a daily basis. Research has shown that one out of six children experiences auditory and tactile sensory symptoms serious enough to negatively impact everyday life.[6] Further research conducted in the USA has shown that one in twenty children experiences sensory processing disorder (SPD),[7] often described as a disorganisation of sensory signals and responses in the brain, affecting different senses. Children with SPD may find it harder to process auditory or tactile stimuli or cope with sensations. This can manifest in either an over- or under-response. For instance, some children may find it very hard to cope with certain fabrics touching their skin, to the point where they find it unbearable. Some may find certain lighting or sounds disturbing and some may not process certain sensations, such as heat and cold, and thus expose themselves to dangerous situations. No one cause of SPD is known; however, it is likely to be a result of a combination of genetics and environmental influences and situations.

Symptoms of SPD are often found on a spectrum, with some more severe than others. As babies and toddlers, children with SPD are often described as 'fussy' or 'very high need'. They can often struggle with sleep and eating and may cry to be held, but then arch away once in their parents' arms. They can also often be extremely active, yet slow to achieve physical milestones; in the toddler years, toilet training can be very difficult. As they grow up, eating and sleeping problems may continue and they can experience more tantrums than average as they strive to cope with stimulation. Body contact with others can be challenging too and they are said to 'over-react' to different experiences. They can often seem to be unco-ordinated and find it hard to master fine motor skills.

Treatment for SPD is multi-faceted and often involves occupational therapy and a therapeutic, sensory-rich environment to help to challenge children in a fun and safe way. Many parents also report success with alternative approaches with complementary therapies. Sensory objects which can help a child to cope on an everyday basis, especially at school, include special 'chewy' jewellery, stress balls and 'fiddle' objects which aid concentration and fulfil their sensory needs in a socially acceptable way.

If you suspect that your child struggles with sensory aspects of life more than their peers, you may want to speak to your GP about the possibility of SPD. There are no specific points at which to explore further; usually your instinct is the best indicator.

Immature verbal communication skills

A child's inability to communicate their feelings and needs verbally can increase the problems created by other triggers; however, it can also be a trigger by itself, even if no others are present.

Can you imagine how it must feel to not be able to communicate your viewpoints, opinions, basic needs and emotions? Even something as simple as letting someone know that you have a headache. Of course, this applies mostly to younger children, although all children can have problems with communication to some degree, whatever their age.

Babies communicate by crying; toddlers too. Tantrums are a classic example of toddler and preschooler communication. In all of these cases language development is lacking and so other methods are resorted to instead. But, you may ask, why don't older children communicate verbally? Surely they have the language abilities to do so? While they may be able to speak or even write fluently, emotional communication remains one of the last skills to develop, and is one that even many adults struggle with. So if we sometimes find it hard to express how we feel, for want of the right words, how can we expect our children to be able to do so? Of course, this presumes that all children are in an environment where expression of feelings is accepted. But many are not. How many times have you heard adults say things like, 'Big boys don't cry', 'You're OK now, stop crying', 'You big sissy', or 'Grow up; stop crying – you're not a little child any more'? Unfortunately, I think these are more common than we would like to believe. We discourage the display of emotions so much in our society, it's no wonder that children struggle to communicate effectively.

One of my favourite sayings is 'All behaviour is communication'. All too often people dismiss unwanted behaviour in children as 'naughty'. Many parenting experts and health professionals advise parents to ignore bad behaviour (and if it is deemed to be 'attention-seeking', this applies even more strongly). I would argue the reverse, however. If a child is desperately seeking parental attention, it makes no sense to ignore them. It is far healthier to give them the attention – remove the cause and you remove the behaviour. Too much parenting advice today disregards the cause of the child's behaviour. If they are feeling a sense of dis-ease, at most you are limited to concealing their discomfort by punishing them for bad behaviour and rewarding them for good. The underlying problem doesn't go away, and it will come back at some point in a different guise.

On the other hand, starting from the position of viewing behaviour as communication of a problem puts parents in a very different position: one of working with their children to solve the problem co-operatively, rather than punishing them for having a problem in the first place.

Psychological behaviour triggers

A lack of control over their own lives

Babies and young children have little to no control over their day-to-day lives. What do they really get to choose for themselves? Do they decide when they go to bed? What they eat?

When they eat? How they spend their day? In most cases the control is in the hands of the parent.

Older children also struggle with a lack of control on an almost daily basis. Parents regulate how they spend their time, what foods they eat, what clothes they wear and even what their rooms look like. Most conversations between parents and children centre around the parent being in charge. This imbalance of power and lack of autonomy for the child can lead to them feeling oppressed, not listened to and angry. The result is the child desperately seeking some control in whatever way that they can, be it shouting, whining, violence, talking back, swearing and tantrums. (Chapters 8, 9, 10 and 13 all explore the link between seeking control and undesirable behaviour.)

Much unwanted behaviour, therefore, can be seen as the child's desperate attempt at regaining some control over their life and asserting their autonomy. Toileting, eating and sleeping issues are most commonly linked to a control problem. Allowing the child to have as much control as possible (age-appropriate and safety allowing) can dramatically change things.

On the flip side there's the idea of boundaries and limits. Giving a child more control does not mean permissive parenting. Children need boundaries and limits to feel safe and to know what is expected of them, and while it is their job to test them, it is our job as adults to set and enforce them. A child raised by a permissive parent can feel very insecure. So deciding on the appropriate boundaries for your family is an important part of parenting, and enforcing them calmly and compassionately is another.

Undesirable behaviour in others

Have you ever heard the saying 'Monkey see, monkey do'? Shouting, swearing and hitting are all behaviours children pick up from us, their peers, other adults, television and other media. If we want to raise kind, polite and calm children, we have to be those things ourselves. If you yell at your children, there is a good chance that they will be yellers. If you smack your children for their wrongdoings, it's likely that they will believe that it is OK to be violent towards others in the name of discipline. If this is the way you yourself were raised, it can be one of the hardest parts of parenting to overcome your own upbringing when it doesn't match up with how you want to raise your children. If you want your children to grow with better qualities than you have, you have to rise above that part of your personality and model the behaviour you wish to see in them. This idea is so important that I have devoted a whole chapter (Chapter 15) to how you can be the person you want your child to be.

Why does your behaviour – and that of others around your child, both young and old – matter? In the 1960s, American psychologist Albert Bandura showed us the important impact of mirroring on children, particularly when it comes to violence, with his infamous 'Bobo Doll' experiment and, later, his theory of Social Learning. Bandura's 1961 experiment involved seventy-two children (thirty-six boys and thirty-six girls) aged between three and six years old. The children were split into one of two experimental groups, each pairing a child and an adult. The first group was known as the 'aggressive modelling' one. Half of the children in this group were paired with an adult of the same sex as them and half with an adult of the opposite sex. The second group was known as the 'non-aggressive modelling' one and, once again, half of the children were paired with an adult of the same sex and half with one of the opposite sex. There was also a control group. All the children were led into a room with their adults. One side of the room contained a craft activity and the other half some small toys, a hammer and an inflatable doll, known as Bobo Doll. In all groups the children were told to not touch the 'adult' toys. In the aggressive group, the accompanying adults hit the Bobo Doll both with their hands and the hammer. In the non-aggressive group, the accompanying adults just played with the small toys and ignored the doll and the hammer. After ten minutes, the children were removed from the room and taken to a new one containing lots of different toys. After two minutes, they were told that they were no longer allowed the toys (this was done in order to build up frustration levels), but could play with the toys in the experiment room. The children were then led back to the original room, this time unaccompanied by an adult. The researchers observed how many times each child was violent towards the Bobo Doll, whether verbally or physically with the hammer.

Unsurprisingly, Bandura and his colleagues found that the children exposed to the aggressive model were more likely to act in physically aggressive ways than those who were in the non-aggressive group. They also found that boys were three times more likely to be violent than girls and both were more likely to be more violent if they were paired with an adult of the same sex. Although now over fifty years old, this experiment still demonstrates the powerful effect of mirroring behaviour. Simply put, we have to be great role models. And, while this research focused on adults and children, the same effect can be true of peer groups. As I said, if we want to raise polite, kind and calm children, it is important that they are around those who exhibit these characteristics.

Lack of connection

Connection, or rather a lack of it, can be the root cause of child behaviour issues at any age. If they are not well connected to you, they are going to try to seek to fix that, often in ways you would rather they didn't. And if they feel a disconnect, they are less likely to want to do things to please you, whether that's tidying their room or getting ready to leave the house at a time you have specified.

Problems with connection can manifest in many different ways. For instance, a toddler starting day care for the first time might cry inconsolably at every drop-off and behave in a way that is deemed 'difficult' in their parents' absence; a preschooler who has just welcomed a new baby sibling could regress in their toileting behaviour; an eight-year-old at school who has busy parents and siblings might compete for parental attention; and a teenager feeling a disconnect because of a disagreement, could ignore their parents' wishes and disobey house rules. All of these situations can be dramatically improved by noting a need for connection and responding with time, love and attention.

Connection is important both in the moment and in the long term. In the short term, the child might 'misbehave' to gain reconnection with you. A young child might hit or kick you in response to not receiving enough attention when you are engaged in a long telephone call, for example. Older children might spend increasing time away from home, ignore curfews, not listen to what you say and get into trouble at school, almost as a way to subconsciously attract your attention. Many parents are tempted to respond by shouting, punishments and sending the child to their room, so compounding the problem by further removing the connection they crave.

One of the most important things you can do as a parent is to nurture – and repair, when necessary – the bond you have with your child. Carefully consider the effects of your discipline and spend time reconnecting on a regular, preferably daily, basis. A fifteen-minute chat at bedtime, ten minutes over breakfast and a quick catch-up in the evening is a great start. In our busy lives, reconnection is often overlooked; ironically, we even sacrifice this special time for taking our children to clubs and classes to aid their development when what they often need most of all is downtime with us. The time when we are exhausted, at the end of our tethers and wondering why we ever had children in the first place is precisely the time when it is vital to reconnect. This will not only help to reduce any further unwanted behaviour in the short term, but will also allow your child to feel that you and they are part of the same team, leading to less unwanted behaviour in the longer term. Children should always feel unconditionally loved by you. You may not like their behaviour, but you love them, and, however angry and exhausted you feel, it is vital that they know this, especially at a time when your reactions may strongly show otherwise.

Childhood deficit – when children aren't allowed to be children enough

Children of all ages need time to be children. They need to play, play, play and play some more. There is plenty of time for children to work, write essays, take tests and use computers and electronic devices later. These things rarely have a true place in childhood, particularly in the early pre-teen years. We are so worried about who they will be tomorrow that we forget to give them time to be children today. This is a huge mistake.

Children, even teens, are not meant to sit still and concentrate for hours on end. They are meant to move and explore the world around them. Play is not a waste of time or something to be done when 'the important stuff' is complete. It *is* the important stuff. Children make sense of their world through play. They learn about scientific concepts, they experiment, they theorise, they work through complicated and often scary and emotional concepts through the safety of play. Take that away and we deprive them of their most important learning skill. In Chapter 5, we will look at education and why it creates so many problems by not meeting the needs of children. The lack of play and understanding of how children learn (discussed in the next chapter) is a major cause of behaviour problems in children today. Never underestimate how important it is for them to climb trees, jump in puddles, swim in the sea and run through fields. These shouldn't be lost at the expense of school tests and homework.

Low self-esteem

It's no coincidence that I am writing about self-esteem just after mentioning education. For a child who is less academically gifted, or one who has trouble 'fitting in' to a system where they must conform and obey, each day brings fresh knocks to their confidence. Success today is too often measured by winning the race, being picked for the team, scoring top marks in tests or producing the best homework. So little emphasis is placed on effort and so much on outcome, and for children who struggle within the system or find it difficult to learn, this is a real problem.

The same is true of 'parent-speak'. Too often we praise success and miss the effort put in, despite frequent failure. When a child has just learned to tie their shoelaces we will often respond with choruses of 'Good boy', 'Well done' or 'Clever girl'. But what about the two hundred times they tried to tie their laces and failed? Didn't they deserve recognition then? Perhaps even more so, for the determination to not give up, despite lack of achievement. This is the approach modern-day discipline methods take as well, as we will see in Chapter 5. In both cases the child's self-esteem is seriously at risk, meaning they begin to think that they are useless, that there is no point in them trying because they can't do better. How do they behave when they feel so bad? In the very ways that we find so difficult.

Once again, we learn that there are many things underlying undesirable behaviour. And the key to effective discipline is to work with the root cause, rather than asserting control, which covers up the problem and solves nothing. Because remember, there is always a reason behind your child's behaviour.

Common misbehaviour myths

While there are many genuine physiological and psychological causes of misbehaviour in children, unfortunately there are also many myths in circulation, and, in order to discipline effectively, it is important that you are aware of these.

Perhaps the greatest misunderstanding in terms of triggers of undesirable behaviour is about the effects of hormones. Have you ever heard that young boys between toddlerhood and age four experience a surge in testosterone? It certainly does seem like a great explanation for the difficult behaviour many parents of young boys face, and I suspect that's why it is so widespread. Unfortunately, however, it's just not true. Testosterone is an important androgen (more commonly known as sex hormone) produced by both males (in the testes and adrenal glands) and females (in the ovaries and adrenal glands). It plays a vital role in bone density and muscle mass, as well as the more obvious development of sexual characteristics. Research has shown that immediately after birth the testosterone levels of boy babies are around 120ng/dl – roughly half the level in an adult male.[8] They then rise fairly significantly to around 260ng/dl between the second and third month, but then begin to fall very quickly. By the time the baby boy is six months old research shows that his testosterone levels will be extremely low and will remain so until he approaches puberty. So the only testosterone spurt that is well documented is the one that occurs in the first few months of life.

Further research backs this up, concluding that 'Statistical analysis did not prove changes in salivary testosterone concentrations in the pre-adolescent period of life, with an exception of the insignificant fall at the age of 7 years, and an insignificant rise at the age of 9 years in girls ... Generally it can be concluded, that salivary testosterone levels in our pre-pubertal subjects remained stable.'[9]

Does this mean that testosterone doesn't *ever* impact behaviour? Not even during and after puberty? Many certainly blame it for many facets of teenage-boy behaviour. Yet research appears to show that the effects, if any, are very minor. In 2014, a systematic review of fifty-three studies was conducted, covering boys aged between nine and eighteen years of age and mostly focused on any relationship between testosterone levels and aggression.[10] The results did not confirm that testosterone levels in boys were related to undesirable behaviour, particularly aggression, with the authors concluding: 'There are insufficient longitudinal data of high methodological quality to currently confirm that changing testosterone levels during puberty are significantly associated with mood and behaviour in adolescent males.' If science does not support a link between testosterone and negative mood and conduct, then what is happening to the tweens and teens who begin acting differently at the onset of puberty? By blaming testosterone, whether the boy is three or thirteen years old, we risk ignoring what is really going on and, in many ways, we fail to discipline correctly as a result.

And what about girls? Does their behaviour change as a result of puberty? Does pre-menstrual syndrome (PMS) play a large role in their attitude? Many parents attribute sassy, irritable and sulky behaviour in teenage girls to 'the time of the month'. Despite this, research appears to show that PMS is not as common as we may believe. A review of forty-seven different studies conducted in New Zealand in 2012 indicated that only 15 per cent of menstruating women experienced classic PMS, with worsening mood in the immediate approach to menstruation and lifted mood once menstruation began.[11] Almost 40 per cent of those studied experienced no menstruation-related mood change and others experienced mood changes after menstruating, rather than before. This begs the question of whether PMS is too often blamed for behaviour in teen girls. Menstruation is viewed very negatively in Western society, with advertisements for products to take the pain and stress of periods away, unfavourable language being used to describe periods and references to irritability in women being due to 'their time of the month'. In many parts of Asia in contrast, it is an accepted part of everyday life, just like any other bodily function. There is no fuss or negativity. Research has found an interesting relationship between culture and PMS. Women in Asia, where PMS isn't such a widely discussed and accepted concept, don't report the same level of issues in the run up to menstruation as do women in Western society.[12] Could it be that PMS is a cultural rather than biological theory? With science finding so few experiencing true PMS, are we potentially missing the real reasons why so many tween and teen girls are frequently irritable and anxious?

Puberty and the teenage years are undoubtedly difficult times. However, this is more likely due to the enormous transition children undergo at this age. So what causes their challenging behaviour? Life. The emotional effects of puberty. The dichotomy of wanting to grow up and become independent, versus the forbidden desire to still be little and nurtured. The tween and teen years throw reality in the face of children far quicker than they are able to handle. The façade and fairy tales of early childhood are shattered and in their place comes the realisation that parents are flawed and the world is actually quite a violent and scary place full of money worries, stress and injustice. Add to this the pressures of school, friendship issues, trying to decide on a future career, anxiety over changing bodies and the onset of periods for girls. Is it any wonder that tweens and teens desperately seek their place in the world and try to assert some control and authority at home and that, as a result, relationships with parents (who often don't look for real reasons and blame behaviour on hormones) suffer? Or, that being bombarded with the negative stereotypes society has of them, they either try to prove them wrong or succumb to them? By attributing our children's undesirable behaviour to hormonal changes we can do them a disservice and often miss the real issues. Separating fact from fiction should always play a role in effective, gentle discipline.

As has become clear in this chapter, understanding and, if possible, avoiding the most common causes of undesirable behaviour in your child is undoubtedly the first step in gentle discipline. Identifying any or all of the triggers that may be at work lays the groundwork for the discipline you will use, helping you to flag up any unmet needs. Once a trigger is removed, the behaviour may naturally be extinguished without any further input from you, although it's not always so simple. Triggers can be very subtle and hard to find, but keeping them in mind, even if they are not obvious, is always a good starting point. And in the following chapters, we will look at what you can do when the cause is either unknown or unavoidable.

Chapter 2

How Children Learn

In this chapter we return to the idea of teaching and learning. Gentle discipline is mindful of the abilities of students. In order to know what our children are capable of learning from discipline, we must understand how they learn. As teachers, we should be aware of the processes involved in their learning, the environment necessary to foster it and how the way that they learn can have implications for how we teach them. Do you remember the list of the attributes a good student needs that I outlined in the Introduction (see page 9)? As we move through this chapter, keep that list in mind. An insight into why certain attributes are necessary for your child to be an effective learner can be very helpful indeed.

There is a misconception in our society that children learn best by being punished and shamed. The reality couldn't be further from the truth. If you want children to behave better, you have to make them feel better.

How would it make you feel if you were chastised and shamed or punished at work? You would likely think your boss was a pretty horrible person and you wouldn't feel motivated to do better, would you? Perhaps you would even think about resigning and finding another job. Children who are punished and shamed feel similarly, I think; only they don't have the luxury of resigning from their family. It is certainly strange that we treat children in ways that we would never put up with ourselves.

Why do most 'parenting experts' only tell you *what* to do, leaving out the 'Why?' Surely that's a more important place to start? To enter the teaching profession, you need to study how children learn long before you can ever begin to teach them. Yet as parents, we are thrown in at the deep end, holding a newborn baby in our arms without a shred of training. Taking some time to understand *how* children learn makes disciplining them infinitely easier, allowing you to improve your teaching and get optimum results.

Abraham Maslow and human motivation[1]

Nobody can learn if their needs are not met: a child who goes to school hungry will find it hard to concentrate; a toddler who is tired will find it hard to take part in their music group; and a child who is very upset will find it hard to listen to you when you speak to them. At a most basic level, we have certain physical and psychological needs that must be addressed in order for learning to take place. Whether this learning happens at home, in the form of discipline, or at school, in the form of education, is irrelevant – the needs remain. So, before we even begin to see how children learn, we must know what these needs are.

In the 1940s, the American psychologist Abraham Maslow devised what he called a 'hierarchy of needs'. He believed that in order to reach their peak potential, individuals had to achieve each level of this hierarchy. If any was omitted, then it was impossible for that individual to 'self-actualise'. Maslow's hierarchy works well when thinking about learning, particularly in children, because it helps us to identify and resolve any unmet needs that may inhibit learning and, indeed, discipline. When it is viewed in the shape of a pyramid, it becomes obvious that we have to first think about how the child feels in order for them to develop the personality traits we hope to see.

A child's hierarchy of needs

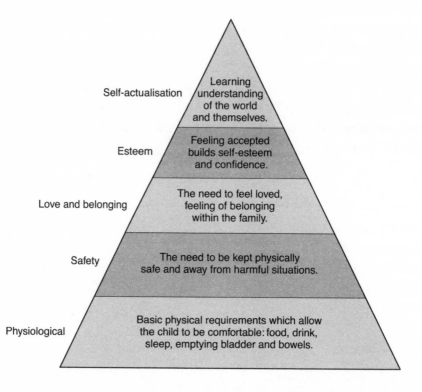

Self-actualisation — Learning understanding of the world and themselves.

Esteem — Feeling accepted builds self-esteem and confidence.

Love and belonging — The need to feel loved, feeling of belonging within the family.

Safety — The need to be kept physically safe and away from harmful situations.

Physiological — Basic physical requirements which allow the child to be comfortable: food, drink, sleep, emptying bladder and bowels.

Starting at the bottom of the hierarchy, children first need their physiological needs met and to be kept safe. Physiological needs, such as food, water, shelter and clothing, are the most basic fulfilments we have in order to survive. Safety focuses on the child being protected from danger and kept away from abuse. Only when these two are satisfied can we move on to the need for love and belonging and then self-esteem. Children have an innate need to be loved and to feel part of a family. Belonging and nurturing help to build not only their self-esteem but also their self-respect, which also helps them to feel a sense of respect towards others. When all these needs are met the child can become the person their parents hope that they will be (actualisation).

Using Maslow's hierarchy, we can see that discipline methods that focus on shaming or punishing via forms of social exclusion (time out, the naughty step and sending to their room, for instance) cannot possibly help to achieve actualisation. You cannot take two sections out of the pyramid and hope to reach the top. A sense of love, belonging and respect are the groundwork for good discipline; the foundation is self-esteem – growing it, rather than destroying it.

Role modelling

In Chapter 1 we looked at Albert Bandura's Bobo Doll experiment (see page 29). Bandura's work clearly showed us that children learn from our example, particularly when it comes to violence. We fail to set good examples to children when we:

- smack them

- shout at them (or other people)

- shame or belittle them (or other people)

- ignore their calls for attention and help

- use bad language towards them (or other people)

- ignore rules and laws

- refuse to share something with somebody

- are rude to somebody.

If we act in any of these ways, we are unwittingly telling our children that not only is it good to behave like this, it's desirable. In effect, discipline is something we do every day. Children watch us more than they listen to us. How you behave today, tomorrow and every day after is setting an example for your child to follow. This is why it is so important to consider my SPACE acronym when you discipline (see page 12). SPACE is largely focused on your behaviour, not that of your child. Remember, you need to stay calm, have appropriate expectations of your child and have an affinity with them before you begin to discipline via connection, containing, explaining and setting an example.

So before we think about changing our children, we should first think about changing ourselves. And this is part of the reason why parenting is so very hard. (We will look at this idea in much more detail in Chapter 15.)

Growth mindset

The American psychologist Carol Dweck is famous for introducing the world to her theory of mindsets and their impact on learning.[2] Mindsets are simply the beliefs we hold about ourselves and our abilities. Dweck describes two distinctly different mindsets: growth and fixed. Growth mindsets are held by people who think that the only limits to their achievements are their efforts. They believe that with hard work and lots of learning they can achieve almost anything that they desire. When they make a mistake, somebody with a growth mindset will not take things personally; they will consider the failure somewhat circumstantial and see it as a learning opportunity, rather than stemming from a lack of ability. Those with a growth mindset tend to be happier and more successful in life. In contrast, those with a fixed mindset believe that their abilities and intelligence are innate and carved in stone. They take failure and mistakes very personally – as a demonstration of their lack of skill – and will give up easily, limiting their own success due to a self-fulfilling prophecy.

Everybody's mindset will be fixed or growth at different times. The two are not mutually exclusive, although, overall, people have a tendency to one more than the other. Which mindset do you believe you have right now when it comes to your child? Analysing your conversations with them can give you a big clue. Do you say things like, 'He's being so naughty, I just feel like giving up – nothing I do seems to make any difference'? Or, 'She's going through a difficult period at the moment – it's hard, but we're still learning and I'm sure we'll get through it.' The first is a good example of a fixed mindset; the latter, a growth mindset. And whichever you believe in is likely to come true.

Can you identify a certain mindset in your child? Which of the following are they more likely to say? 'I'm so bad at maths – it's not even worth me trying. I'm going to fail the test anyway.' Or, 'Riding a bike is tricky isn't it? I keep falling off, but I think I'll be able to do it if I keep trying.'

Which mindset do you think makes for good discipline? Encouraging children, especially when they make mistakes and poor choices, promotes a growth mindset. Punishment, in contrast, keeps children in a fixed state of mind. They begin to believe they are 'naughty' or 'stupid' and, ultimately, they give up trying because they accept that they are what people call them. When it comes to discipline, a growth mindset teaches children that they can be and do better – that doing something wrong today doesn't mean they can't do something great tomorrow. It improves their motivation and, as a result, their behaviour.

It is important to understand, however, that praise, as well as punishment and shaming, can have a negative effect. Do you ever praise your child for being 'clever' or 'bright'? By praising an innate ability you may accidentally push your child into a more fixed mindset. To foster a growth mindset you should only praise either something that can be changed or your child's effort: 'I saw you tried really hard with that puzzle. You didn't finish it, but that's OK, I'm sure you'll do it next time.' Praise can be quite a tricky discipline tool. We will look at it in more detail in Chapter 4.

Learning styles

Do you remember how you learned best at school? Writing endless notes? Making up mnemonics to remember facts? Watching plays or videos? While the idea of learning styles is controversial, and indeed some don't believe in it, I think it can be useful when considering discipline. Most mainstream discipline focuses on auditory learning, with the parent giving verbal instructions (often repeatedly). This can work well if the child is an auditory learner, but what if they are not? Is the problem theirs for not suiting the style of discipline their parent uses? Or should the parent change their approach to accommodate the individual needs of their child?

In the VARK model, education expert Neil Fleming describes four main learning styles that apply to children:

- Visual

- Auditory

- Read/write

- Kinesthetic[3]

Children will all be a mix of each style, but usually one will predominate, and may change over time.

Visual

Visual learners learn best through seeing. They learn well with pictures and images and graphic information. They tend to excel in art, photography and film and love to draw and experiment with colour. Visual learners do well when asked to imagine what something looks like, drawing mind maps and diagrams to explain situations. Visualisations work well for them and they can often picture things in their minds that others can't.

Auditory

Auditory learners learn best through hearing. They respond well to listening to other people talking and to any learning associated with music. They tend to excel in singing or playing an instrument and have strong emotions in reaction to music. Auditory learners do well when they are asked to use sound in a task, such as making up a mnemonic or a rhyme.

Read/write

Read/write learners learn best through words. They often have a great love of reading and write many notes. This style is often described as having 'a way with words'. Read/write learners do best when they are asked to read or write about something.

Kinesthetic

Kinesthetic learners learn best through touching, doing and moving. They are 'hands on' and like to touch whatever they are learning about, rather than reading instructions. They usually excel in sports and love to move. They are the people who 'never stay still'. They also like to make models. They do best when allowed the movement they need, which can help to calm them down, and when movement and gestures are part of their learning.

Which do you think is your child's predominant learning style? Observing your child's behaviour can really help you to understand their learning style, and once you've done this, you can tailor your discipline so that it's significantly more effective.

If you have a kinesthetic learner, for example, there is no point giving them over-lengthy explanations about what they did wrong and what they should do next time; however, they may respond really well to a role play. Visual learners, in contrast, would learn very little from a role play but could benefit from drawing a mind map with you, to look at other ways they could behave next time. A read/write learner would most likely not learn well from a mind map but could respond very well to communication through little notes left in their bedroom and in yours in response. Lastly, an auditory learner may shy away from notes but would probably love to make up a song with you to help them to behave better next time.

Here are some discipline ideas based on different learning styles:

Visual

- Draw simple diagrams or cartoons to show your child better ways to behave.

- Encourage them to draw pictures to show their emotions.

- Use visualisations to help calm your child down.

Auditory

- Make up a song to cope in certain situations, for instance a nappy-change song.

- Make up acronyms or mnemonics to help them to remember how to respond in tricky situations, for example ABC for 'Always Be Calm'.

- Use relaxation music to help them to calm down.

Read/write

- Find special books to help your child understand their own emotions and those of others.

- Suggest they keep a diary, recording their feelings in it each night.

- Write special notes to each other, explaining how you both feel.

Kinesthetic

- Role-play what happened and how your child could respond differently.

- Encourage them to clean up or fix whatever they ruined with you.

- Go for a walk together to discuss what happened.

Working with, rather than against, your child's learning style almost always provides the most effective discipline. And the more fun and creative your solution, the better. Most people have more than one style, so don't be afraid to try a mixture of different approaches – if something doesn't work, move on and try the next one. Remember, you're aiming for a growth mindset!

Experiential learning and schemas

Children learn by experience. Or, more specifically, they learn when they reflect on something they do or did. We can tell them of our experiences and we can give them advice, but they only truly learn when they go through something them-selves. The idea of experiential learning is ancient. In 350BC Aristotle said, 'For the things we have to learn before we can do them, we learn by doing them.' And, in terms of discipline, we once again return to the idea of being a good role model. If we want to raise respectful, kind and polite children, we must be that way with them. Children do not learn to be respectful in an environment in which they are disrespected. They do not learn to be kind if they are not treated kindly. They learn by doing, reflecting, then doing again with previous experi-ence in mind.

Have you ever wondered why your child does something, even when you've told them not to do it and explained why they shouldn't? Perhaps your three-year-old insisted on touching the hot oven door, despite you telling him he shouldn't. Being told something will happen when you do something and doing it yourself are two very different things. It is only when the child touches the oven door and experiences the heat that he truly understands and learns.

In the 1950s the Swiss philosopher Jean Piaget introduced us to the idea of schemas, which he described as 'a cohesive, repeatable action sequence possessing component actions that are tightly interconnected and governed by a core meaning'. Put simply, he considered schemas to be the building blocks of knowledge – how children think and, ultimately, learn. Piaget believed that a child forms schemas based on their experience of life. For instance, if they encountered a little girl with blonde hair who was mean, they might presume that all little girls with blonde hair are mean. It is only through repeated experience and exposure that they learn that some people are mean, regardless of gender, hair colour and age. Over time, the child builds more and more elaborate schemas, until they reach a point of cognitive comfort or, in other words, a good understanding of the world around them. Until then, however, they might, justifiably, experience a degree of puzzlement and discomfort.

Confusingly, the word schema is used elsewhere in child development, in a way that is unrelated to Piaget's theory. This other meaning describes a repetitive pattern in the behaviour of young children, and is used frequently among early-years educators and childcare professionals. Specific individual schemas, largely noted in children's play, are identified, including the following:

Connection schema

In this schema children learn how to connect things. They will often be engrossed in building train tracks, sticking building blocks together or laying pieces of paper on the floor to make a path.

Containing schema

The containing schema occurs when children place objects into a container of some form. For instance, they may put all of their crayons into an empty bag or inside a large box.

Enveloping schema

In this schema children learn to cover things up. For instance, they may cover their teddy bear with a blanket or their food with a napkin.

Positioning schema

Here, children are learning about the position of one object in relation to another. They will often move their food around to different positions on the plate or they may want to sit in a different place from where they have been instructed to.

Rotation schema

This schema is all about objects rotating. Children may be engrossed in watching the washing machine or the motion of wheels turning. They will often try to turn things that they think may rotate, such as the hands of a clock or a ball on the floor.

Trajectory schema

This schema teaches children about movement and direction: throwing things, say, food from their high chair or water into the air, to observe their trajectory.

Transforming schema

This relates to the changing properties of objects. Children will pour their juice into their porridge and explore the resulting transformation with their fingers. Or they may pour sand from their sand pit into their hair to feel the change in texture.

Transporting schema

This looks at children moving objects from one place to another – for instance, moving cans stacked in a cupboard to a different area of the kitchen or pushing a cart containing building blocks from one part of the garden to another.

Not surprisingly, many of these schemas can be problematic for parents. The child's learning is often at odds with social rules and expectations and can be very messy. But while you would much rather your child didn't pour juice in their dinner, empty a packet of baby wipes and put them all into the toilet bowl or rearrange the contents of your kitchen cupboard, you can rest assured that not only are these behaviours and others like them totally normal, they are also quite positive and indicative of great learning.

Good learning environment

If we want children to learn well, we need to provide them with an environment that nurtures that process. And the same applies to gentle discipline. When we teach our children to behave in more appropriate ways, we must consider the environment in which we do so.

What does a good learning environment look like? Physically speaking, it should be uncluttered, yet inspiring. It should allow the child to have a good degree of autonomy, with learning tools placed at their level, so that they can reach them independently. Most importantly of all though, the environment should be calm and supportive. The child should be made to feel a sense of belonging. In fact, Maslow's hierarchy of needs applies here: their environment should be calm and supportive, with an understanding and well-informed teacher who is available to listen and explain things whenever needed. Disciplining in a state of anger, ignoring the child's needs or excluding them from you is never effective, just as it is not in an educational setting.

Disciplining in a compassionate way that takes account of the child's self-esteem – and with a growth mindset and an understanding of your child's learning style and what they need to reach their full potential – is the epitome of gentle discipline. It is also vital to have a good grasp of their behavioural capabilities at each age, a topic covered in some depth in the next chapter.

Chapter 3

How Children's Brains Develop

Society today takes the view that children who misbehave are being deliberately naughty – that they plot and scheme to get what they want and make a conscious decision to behave in ways we dislike. But what if they behave undesirably, not deliberately, but because they cannot do anything else?

As I've said, most common discipline methods focus on encouraging children to do and be better, so that they are motivated by rewards if they behave 'well' and punishments if they misbehave. This would seem sensible, but it makes one huge mistake. It presumes that the child is not motivated to be 'good' and that they have the capability to change their behaviour. But maybe they already have the motivation? Maybe they already want to do better? And perhaps their brains – their capabilities – are holding them back? Are they behaving in a certain way simply because they cannot behave in any other? Mainstream discipline methods can achieve absolutely nothing here, except make the child feel worse.

Gentle discipline starts from the position of ensuring that

what we expect of our children is appropriate for their age and abilities. In this chapter we will take a look at some of the most common emotional skills and when we can expect our children to have reached a level similar to those of an adult. This understanding of our child's neurology aids us in our discipline efforts, not only in terms of our expectations – are we punishing the child for simply having a child's brain? – but also in the form of discipline we select. The most effective methods are those that take into account the child's cognitive abilities. Far too many mainstream approaches do not do this.

How the brain develops

When a baby is born they have 200 billion neurons and their brain is around 30 per cent of the size of an adult's. Each day it grows by around one and a half grams and by the age of two it will have reached 75 per cent of its full size. In order to aid this fast growth, over half of the baby's energy intake, from milk, is used by the brain.

During the first three years of life, around seven hundred new neural connections, or synapses, are made in the brain every single second. These connections serve as the 'wiring' for the brain. By the time a child is three years old they have formed over one thousand trillion synapses. These connections – formed through a combination of genetics and life experience – are of great significance to the future brain architecture and have a significant impact in adulthood. As such, the environment a child lives in, including their relationships with their main carers, can have as much influence on their brain development as genetics. Ultimately, these connections, or rather those that are not regularly reinforced, are removed by a process called neural pruning. The term 'use it or lose it' has a special significance here. By the teenage years, the connections in the brain have already dropped from one thousand trillion to five hundred trillion, after which they remain relatively stable throughout the adult years. While it is still possible to form new neural connections at any age, it is much harder in adulthood, particularly when it comes to changing behaviour, compared with the early years. The same is true of neural pruning, which continues throughout life, but not to the extent to which it occurs in childhood.

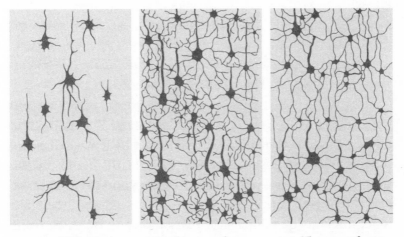

at a child's birth   *at 7 years of age*   *at 15 years of age*

So, for their brains to develop to their full potential, children need an environment of support, a variety of enriching experiences and love. Those who lack these undergo something known as 'toxic stress'. The physiological responses caused by repeatedly elevated stress levels negatively impact the development of the brain and, in this instance, the neural connections most affected are those in the higher cognitive function sections, such as critical and analytical thought, as well as impulse control and emotion regulation.

At birth, babies are very sensory, with the areas of the brain responsible for sight, hearing, smell, touch and taste relatively well connected. These senses allow them to stay safe and to bond with their parents. They also allow them to experience the world, with new sensory events providing enrichment that further develops the brain. In the early years, the brain functions well in the most primitive parts. At birth, the baby's brainstem is well developed, keeping their body systems regulated – a process known as homoeostasis. The baby's temporal lobe and limbic system, responsible for emotions and hearing, function fairly well too, as do their occipital lobe, responsible for sight, and their cerebellum, which is responsible for movement. In addition, the baby's parietal lobe, responsible for touch and language, is quite well developed. The connections in these parts of the brain grow throughout baby- and toddlerhood and mature as the child reaches school age.

In contrast, the frontal lobe and prefrontal cortex remain immature until late adolescence. The frontal lobe is the first of the two to mature and is linked with problem solving and sorting and categorising to make sense of the world. By the time a child is twelve years of age we can expect this part of the brain to be well connected. The very last section of the brain to mature, during the teenage years and early twenties, is the prefrontal cortex, which controls judgement, impulse control and emotion regulation. Until this section of the brain is well connected, it is reasonable to expect the child, or indeed teenager, to lack judgement and self-control.

Developing emotion regulation

Regulating our emotions is quite a mature skill. As adults, we may be able to press the pause buttons in our brains when we are tempted to shout, swear or act violently towards somebody. If we feel anxious or scared, we may be able to talk ourselves out of our emotional discomfort by rationalising and diffusing our feelings. Children, however, do not have these skills – at least not to the same level as adults. And this difference in emotion-regulation ability is the cause of a lot of stress for parents who expect their children to have the same capabilities that they do. In fact, self-regulation takes years to develop, and getting to know why your child lashes out, when you yourself are able to stay calm, is another of the foundations of gentle discipline.

Impulse control

Imagine that you are in a shop full of row upon row of designer handbags or a showroom full of sports cars. You can smell the leather of the handbags and they have your favourite style in twenty different colours, each one seemingly calling your name; or rows of shiny, sparkling new sports cars that are begging to be driven, their paintwork so immaculate it reflects your image back at you and you just know the engines would roar like a proud lion. What would be your first instinct? I'll bet you would want to stroke the bags and inhale the scent of newness. Or perhaps you would want to put your hand on a car's bonnet, just imagining the power underneath. Touch is so important when shopping. When did you last buy an item of clothing without first touching it to feel the fabric, for example?

Now imagine you are three years old and you are in the glass department of a large department store. Each delicate object is glinting under the lighting tracks, throwing rainbows in every direction. How much would you want to touch these beautiful things? Perhaps you would break away from your parents while they were distracted and feel the cool smoothness of glass under your palm. Then, oops, you're a little too rough and the store is filled with the sound of shattering glass. Or perhaps your parents spot you before you can get to them, and they shout 'Don't touch!' and pull you away.

There is very little difference in the two scenarios, aside from it being much harder to break handbags and sports cars. The captivating beauty of things we cannot have affects us at any age. Three-year-olds, however, have the added disadvantage of a biological lack of impulse control. For them, every day is filled with forbidden fruit. Just think how frustrating it must be to be told 'No' over and over – to be overwhelmed, out of control and surrounded by temptation when you simply cannot manage your response. It's not surprising that they want to sneakily touch things, is it?

Related to impulse control is the idea of the dominant response. This is an almost automatic, unconscious response to a stimulus – and it is the most common and quickest one. In babies it is clearly crying. In toddlers it could be argued to be crying or having a tantrum. In older children it may be whining or crying, while in teenagers it could be shouting or physical displays of anger. The reason that this is related to impulse control is that it is almost impossible for a child, from newborn to teen, to override their dominant response and react in a more socially acceptable way if they do not have adequate impulse control. Sometimes, children who always shout or cry just simply cannot help it.

Critical, analytical, abstract and hypothetical thought

As adults we are able to analyse our own thoughts and work to calm ourselves down when we are anxious, scared, angry, overwhelmed, sad and stressed. We are usually able to diffuse our feelings using a mix of critical, analytical and hypothetical thought. To think critically and analytically means considering a scenario, why it happened, how others felt, how we reacted and whether that reaction was appropriate, without having to rely on actual experience to be able to do so. Hypothetical and abstract thought means that we are able to reflect on what may happen in the future as a result of our own or somebody else's actions. It is the lack of these sophisticated thought processes that are the cause of many emotional meltdowns and undesirable behaviour in children of all ages.

A good analogy for an emotional meltdown – or tantrum, if we are talking about toddlers – is to imagine a pot of water on a stove. The gas is on full and the water soon begins to boil. Soon it is boiling over, spilling down the sides of the pot. The gas is still on full, so the water continues to boil until the pot runs dry. That's a meltdown or tantrum. Left to their own devices, perhaps in time out or on a naughty step, a child's 'pot' will continue to boil over until either the source is exhausted or the child is so drained that they are 'empty'. Some may think time out and naughty steps – or any other 'discipline' method where the child's feelings and behaviour are ignored (in the false belief that this will stop it happening again) are effective. Yet how can the child learn anything, which is the true goal of discipline, if they are left to 'boil over' and run dry?

Time out or the naughty step (which are essentially one and the same, with or without the addition of a designated step, stool or chair) rely on punishing the child's wrongdoings by excluding them from those they love. The idea is that while they are excluded they are to consider what they have done wrong, how they made the wronged party feel and how they can behave better next time. Once they have done this and are calm, they are allowed to leave the exclusion area. It sounds so simple, doesn't it? But most children who are socially excluded are between the ages of two and ten and neuroscience shows that at any of these ages a child is not capable of the complex thought that the discipline method requires. In order for them to analyse their behaviour and hypothesise about how they may behave in future they have to have a firm grasp of concrete thinking – or, rather, they need a good level of critical, analytical and hypothetical thought. These thought processes are all the domain of the frontal lobe of the brain, which, as we discussed earlier, is not mature until just before a child enters their teenage years.

Children find it hard to think logically in an abstract manner – that is, without visual clues to manipulate – until they reach, on average, their eleventh birthday. It is only at this point that their thought processes become more adult-like in terms of their problem-solving abilities and capacity to think critically. The facility to manipulate and predict different outcomes via hypothetical thought is perhaps one of the last 'adult' thought processes to appear. Without an appropriate level of neural connectivity in the frontal, thinking part of the brain a child is incapable of the thought processes demanded by time out and the naughty step. They cannot (and do not) analyse their behaviour and consider future outcomes. At best, they will sit or stand quietly because they have learned that it is the only way they are allowed to rejoin their friends and loved ones.

The development of empathy

Empathy is the ability to recognise and identify with the feelings and emotions of others. Those who are empathic are more likely to display prosocial or altruistic behaviours. Empathy begins to develop from birth, through a mix of experience and brain maturation; however, it does not reach levels comparable to those found in adults until the child is of school age. A lack of empathy in very young children is, therefore, to be expected.

A toddler who struggles with sharing, for example, is entirely normal. Very often, even if a child is upset and in tears, the child who is refusing to share will be unable to empathise with the other child's feelings or to understand the consequences of their own actions. Recognising this, we quickly realise that there is little point in reprimanding a child for not sharing.

Around the mid-twentieth century, the Swiss philosopher Jean Piaget introduced the concept of egocentrism[1] – a developmentally normal psychological stage that children pass through which explains their inability to understand the thoughts and feelings of other people. (It is important here to distinguish this from being egotistical, which is an undesirable adult personality trait.) Piaget believed that all children under the age of seven are extremely egocentric, and that it is only between the ages of seven and twelve that they begin to slowly move away from that position. Others believe that egocentrism is still present after this,[2] while research with university students[3] has also shown that egocentrism is evident in the late teens, and that girls are more egocentric than boys. (It could be argued that a sense of egocentrism in teens could help with developing a sense of self-identity.)

In the late 1970s, two psychologists, David Premack and Guy Woodruff, took the idea of egocentrism further, introducing the idea of Theory of Mind (ToM), which is reliant on the child's brain development and maturation, and means that they begin to understand that not everybody thinks and feels the same as them. So, until their ToM is sufficiently developed, it is extremely difficult for children to appreciate the consequences of their actions. (Premack and Woodruff also famously questioned whether chimpanzees possess a ToM.)

Several famous experiments followed this work, including the 'Sally Ann test', which focused on the theory of 'false belief' as a way of testing for ToM.[4] It involved introducing children to two dolls, named Sally and Ann. The children were asked to recall the dolls' names, and were then shown Sally 'leaving' the room. While she was away, Ann removed a marble from

Sally's bag and hid it in her own box. Sally then returned and the children were asked, 'Sally wants her marble. Where will she look for it?'

The correct answer, in that it is the one that shows an understanding of Sally's beliefs, is obviously that it's in her bag, as Sally doesn't know that Ann has moved the marble. Eighty-five per cent of children under four, however, will answer this question incorrectly, saying Sally will look for the marble in Ann's box – what the researchers term as 'false belief'. This simple experiment shows clearly that young children struggle to put themselves in another person's shoes, due to their undeveloped ToM or empathy.

Crucial changes in ToM happen at around four years of age, when children begin to be able to interpret accurately the contents of others' minds, especially their belief states. It is at this stage that we can expect their behaviour to be more empathic and prosocial. Put simply, we should not expect a child to share until they have reached school age. Readjusting our expectations of children, even in their teens, is incredibly important.

So how does empathy develop? The more empathic and respectful we are towards them, the more children will grow to be that way with others. The concept of mind-mindedness illustrates this idea well. Mind-mindedness is simply a parent or carer's ability to be empathic towards their child, and to understand that they have important feelings of their own. Research has shown that mothers who are more mind-minded raise children with a better-established ToM and greater levels of empathy.[5] This is where it is important to revisit the idea of punishing a child for not sharing. Any punishment displays a lack of empathy from the adult's perspective and often a lack of understanding of normal child development. When we consider that unempathic behaviour is likely to foster the same in a child, it becomes clear that we need to find other ways of managing issues such as children sharing.

Risk taking

Have you ever wondered why teenagers do so many stupid things? Have you ever been driving and a thirteen-, fourteen- or fifteen-year-old has run in front of your car?

Two-thirds of children involved in road-traffic accidents when on foot are boys, while the age group most frequently involved is twelve- to fifteen-year-olds. Why is this? First, research indicates that the male hormone testosterone increases risk-taking behaviour, making boys more likely to engage in risky behaviour than girls. [6] And second, teenagers' brains have the engine of a sports car, but the brakes of a mini.

The teenage brain is drawn to risky situations and often shows little regard for safety; it is wired in such a way that teens do not perceive risk in the same way as adults. From their point of view, this is a good thing. It helps them to learn, develop and grow, particularly their brains. From their parents' point of view, however, it is the cause of a great deal of anxiety. Research has shown that teenagers are more likely to engage in risky behaviour if the activity has an unknown risk to them – i.e. they don't know what the potential outcomes are or why it could be dangerous. [7] When the risk is known, however, they are less likely to engage in risky behaviour than adults. This is likely to be due to the way the teen brain processes information. The development of rational thinking happens before that of hypothetical thinking, meaning that teens can process and act on a risk assessment of something they know about, for instance safe sex. When the risk is unknown, however, they find it much harder to hypothesise than adults do. Allowing teens to think about and experience risk in a safe and supervised situation seems to be the most obvious way to help them to stay safe.

Deviations from neuro-typical behaviour

As we have learned, children's brains are different from adults', and this presents many challenges to us as parents. Sometimes, when the child's brain differs from the norm, these challenges can be even more pronounced. In these cases, the child's behaviour may require very specific attention, as different disorders might be indicated. The three that tend to impact the most are attention deficit hyperactivity disorder, oppositional defiant disorder and autistic-spectrum disorders. These disorders are the most common when it comes to considering non neuro-typical behaviour. Let's look briefly at each of them in turn.

Attention deficit hyperactivity disorder (ADHD)

ADHD is characterised by inconsistent attention. Common symptoms include prolonged periods of restlessness, fidgeting, impulsivity and becoming easily distracted. These may be noticeable at any age, but most children are diagnosed between the ages of six and twelve. ADHD is widely researched and discussed and yet it remains something of an enigma. Research has shown a large disparity between the UK and the USA in the number of diagnoses of ADHD, with the USA reporting four or five times more than the UK in relation to population size.[8] Does this mean that more children are affected in the USA? Unlikely. The most realistic answer is that the diagnosis is made far more freely in the USA, although in both countries rates of ADHD are on the rise. (In the USA between 7 and 11 per cent of children are diagnosed with ADHD, while in the UK this figure is closer to 2 per cent.)

There is some controversy surrounding the diagnosis of ADHD. Some believe it is a psychological disorder, often the result of 'poor parenting', while others believe it does not exist at all and the difficult behaviour is due to poor diet or an oppressive education system and is, as such, a culturally created problem. The current evidence-based view, however, is that ADHD has a biological cause, based in the brain. This neuro-logical variation results in the child developing a difference in cognition from that which is neuro-typical.

Research involving brain imaging of adults who were diagnosed with ADHD as children, some of whom still suffer from the effects, found that there was a significant difference in the default-mode networks between those who still had ADHD symptoms and those who did not.[9] The default-mode network is a system in the brain, comprised of several related areas, that is more active when a person is not focused on what is going on around them and is in a daydream-type state. Those subjects who no longer showed symptoms had default-mode networks similar to people who had never suf-fered from ADHD. Further studies using brain imaging show that the metabolism of the brain is lower in the cerebellum and prefrontal cortex areas of the brain that control move-ment, attention and judgement.[10] The brains of children with ADHD were shown to be 5 per cent smaller when compared with children who were not affected. Lastly, children with ADHD were shown to have lowered levels of dopamine, a chemical that transmits signals in the brain. Among other functions, dopamine is involved in motor control. This means that a child with ADHD often moves around a lot more than neuro-typical children, and is likely to struggle in situations where they are required to sit still and quietly, due to their impaired impulse control. Children with ADHD may require specialist insight and interventions from medical and therapeutic teams in addition to parental discipline.

Oppositional defiant disorder (ODD)

Children diagnosed with ODD frequently display angry, vindictive and irritable behaviour. They also tend to be argumentative and defiant towards people in authority.

ODD commonly occurs in families where there is a history of ADHD and other mood disorders, although whether this indicates a genetic or environmental cause remains unknown. ODD may possibly result in injuries or deformities in the brain, although not enough research exists to support or refute this. As with ADHD, there may also be an abnormal functioning of neurotransmitters in the brain. Research has found that there is an atypical activation pattern in the frontal section of the brain, which is responsible for socially acceptable behaviour, impulse control and judgement.[11] For a diagnosis to be made, the child must have exhibited the defiant behaviour for at least six months.

Autism-spectrum disorders (ASD)

It is estimated that eleven in every thousand people will be on the autistic spectrum. There is no known cause of ASD, although a mix of genetic and environmental factors is likely to be at work.

Autism is characterised by difficulties with both verbal and non-verbal communication, struggles with social interactions and behaviour that is often repetitive. In children, signs usually begin to show within the first two years. In babies and toddlers, potential signs of autism include:

- avoiding eye contact

- a lack of babbling

- not using or responding to facial expressions, such as smiling

- not gesturing or picking up on gestures, such as waving

- not imitating facial expressions, sounds or words

- a dislike of being held and cuddled and not reaching to be picked up

- not engaging in play with people

- not following somebody else's gaze or pointing

- not responding to their name

- not making noises, or crying, to get parental attention

- not speaking or using words.

Children with autism can also really struggle to sleep and have very disturbed sleeping patterns. They may find it incredibly hard to settle in the first place or they may wake frequently throughout the night; or they may have problems with both. There may be issues with their behaviour too, particularly in a social context, and they may display what many people consider to be 'bad' or 'naughty' behaviour as a result. Lastly, they can have difficulties with under- or overeating, which is often related to sensory issues. Autism can also be accompanied by learning disabilities.

Many different brain areas and functions are affected in autism and there is no clear neurological pattern. Research suggests that these brain differences begin very early in life, likely before birth.[12] Scientists have found that immediately post birth the brains of babies with autism grow faster than average; however, the growth then slows during childhood.[13]

They have also speculated whether autism is due to an excess or unusual movement of neurons[14] or an abnormal formation of synapses – or connections – in the brain. Among many other hypotheses, it is also thought that the neurotransmitter serotonin may also play a role.[15] The likelihood is that there is a multitude of different neurological causes of autism, combined with other physiological factors.

Asperger syndrome

Asperger syndrome is a form of autism. People with Asperger syndrome struggle with social skills, particularly communication, interaction and imagination. They will often find understanding conversations, facial expressions and other body language difficult, as well as jokes and irony. Sometimes, those with Asperger syndrome fail to recognise social niceties, such as not interrupting a conversation or making 'small talk', although they tend to have fewer problems with speaking than those with autism and do not usually experience the same learning disabilities. Children with Asperger syndrome may also experience sensory difficulties (both over- and under-reactive) and issues with living spontaneously (without following a rigid routine) and can sometimes form intense interests and obsessions.

Pathological demand avoidance (PDA)

Like those with Asperger syndrome, people with PDA can struggle with social situations and communications. However, they tend to have more of an understanding and better execution of communication skills. They may struggle with expectations and demands, usually when they are feeling anxious because of a lack of control. Because of this, they may find everyday life challenging and can often behave compulsively and obsessively and suffer with mood swings. The personality of somebody with PDA can seem quite controlling and dominating, usually at times when they are feeling anxious; however, on the flip side, they can be incredibly enigmatic, usually at times when their anxiety is lessened. Like autism and Asperger syndrome, PDA is likely to be caused by differences in the brain and genetics in combination with environmental factors.

Parenting a child who is not neuro-typical can be very challenging, especially when it comes to discipline, so if you suspect that this is the case for your child, do visit your family doctor and ask for their help and advice. Gentle discipline is appropriate for all children, but sometimes you will need specialist insight and input if your child has a specific condition. There are many organisations that can provide help and support – you will find some of them listed in the resources section on page 266.

Understanding how children's brains develop is one of the cornerstones of gentle discipline. Unfortunately, many of today's most common discipline methods are not mindful of this stage in a child's life – something we will explore in more detail in the next chapter. Effective gentle discipline should always consider the child's current level of cognitive ability, both when looking for the cause of their behaviour and when seeking an appropriate response.

Chapter 4

The Problem with Common Discipline Methods

It should be clear by now that many of the common discipline techniques used today are mindful of neither neurological development nor learning. Much of the parenting advice given when children misbehave seeks only to control their behaviour in the moment, not to find out the reasoning behind it. The results are quick and the parental effort needed to achieve them is fairly small – and this is where the appeal lies – but it's a short-sighted approach, and little thought is given to the effects on the child in ten, twenty or thirty years' time. As with anything in life, quick fixes usually come with risks. Crash diets, for example, have been proven to not only be unhealthy but to cause you to gain more weight in the long run. The same is true of quick-fix discipline – the long-term effects are not worth any short-term gain.

As we have discussed, gentle discipline is all about effective teaching and learning, putting SPACE between your child's actions and your reactions (see page 12) and being mindful about how your discipline will help to mould the individual you hope your child will grow into in the years to come. In this chapter, therefore, I will look at some of the most common discipline techniques used today, their pitfalls and if there is any potential for them to be used more gently and effectively. Specific behaviour scenarios are examined in the chapters that follow.

Ineffective quick-fix discipline methods

Let's start by looking at common methods that have no place at all in gentle discipline. These are not only ineffective in the long term, but may also prove damaging and cause more difficult behaviour in the future. They are diametrically opposed to what you hope to do by parenting mindfully and respectfully.

Punishments, ignoring and isolation and rewards are the mainstay of many popular parenting techniques. Let's look at why they are a poor form of discipline.

The problem with punishment

Good teachers inspire children to improve themselves by giving them confidence. When children are punished they don't feel encouraged to do better. Instead, they feel a disconnect with their parents: 'If my mother loved me, she wouldn't hit me, shout at me or send me upstairs.' In Chapter 1, we discussed how this can be a trigger for poor behaviour. It makes no sense to discipline by making children feel more disconnected – all this does is increase the potential for more undesirable behaviour by making them feel worse.

To children, the way you act towards them is a clear demonstration of your love for them. Treat them badly and they often assume that you no longer care about them. This feeling is compounded by punishments that hinge on social exclusion, such as time out or the naughty step. The unwanted behaviour may cease temporarily, but temporary it is. Plus, no true learning has taken place. All the child has learned, through a process of conditioning, is that your punishment is associated with a certain behaviour and to avoid the punishment they should avoid the behaviour. But they have not learned how to handle a situation more effectively, to be more sociable or to have better morals and more respect for you. Punishment teaches nothing but fear, and once the fear of the threatened punishment wears off, the behaviour returns, or resurfaces in a slightly different way. Also, while it is fairly easy to punish small children, when they approach their teens and begin to tower over you it is no longer so effective.

Classical and operant conditioning

Much mainstream discipline works via a process of either classical or operant conditioning. Both are processes of association, but neither prompts an underlying change in belief or a desire to change in children.

Classical conditioning

Classical conditioning is an effect discovered by the psychologist Ivan Pavlov. It explains the learning of a new behaviour by the process of association in three distinct stages:

- **Stage 1:** this involves an unconditioned stimulus (UCS) and an unconditioned response (UCR). These produce a natural, non-learned response. For example, jumping on a trampoline may cause a child to laugh. Stage 1 also includes something known as a neutral stimulus (NS), something that naturally has no effect. For instance, a garden alone may not elicit a response unless it is accompanied by the unconditioned stimulus, in this case the trampoline.

- **Stage 2:** this involves the neutral stimulus being paired with the unconditioned stimulus. This then becomes known as a conditioned stimulus (CS). It is likely to take several repetitions, however, for the stimulus to become conditioned.

- **Stage 3:** the conditioned stimulus becomes associated with the unconditioned stimulus and now forms a conditioned response. In the case of laughter, trampolines and gardens, the child will now laugh when they are in a garden, even in the absence of a trampoline.

When related to parenting, we can see how classical conditioning can elicit a behaviour (the conditioned response). However, this does not occur because of a change of motivation or a true understanding of the impact of their behaviour. Based on this, it could be argued that discipline that relies on classical conditioning is not effective or appropriate.

Operant conditioning

Psychologist B. F. Skinner believed that classical conditioning was too simplistic and did not adequately explain the behaviour of humans. He claimed that it was better to look at the causes of a certain behaviour and any consequences. This is known as operant conditioning.

Operant conditioning argues that behaviour that is reinforced is strengthened and that which is not reinforced is extinguished. It is these responses, or what he called operants, that interested Skinner. He described three types of operant:

- **Neutral operants** These responses, from the environment or other people, have a neutral effect. They do not strengthen or extinguish a behaviour.

- **Reinforcers** These responses, from the environment or other people, increase the likelihood that a behaviour will be repeated.

- **Punishers** These responses, from the environment or other people, decrease the likelihood that a behaviour will be repeated.

In the case of childhood behaviour, we commonly use reinforcers, in the form of rewards, and punishers, in the form of punishment. In both cases, the responses elicit an extrinsically motivated response from the child – that is, behaviour manipulated by external factors. Extrinsically motivated behaviour, such as that derived from operant conditioning, is good for short-term compliance. It is only when behaviour is intrinsically motivated however – when the motivation comes from within the child and they learn *how* to do better – that we see long-lasting change.

Physical punishment

Physical punishment, sometimes known as corporal punishment, fits very much into the 'punisher' class of operant conditioning. Parents who advocate smacking, spanking, tap-ping, popping or any other name used to try to make the act sound less aggressive, claim that it teaches children respect. Think back to our definition of a 'good teacher' though: do you think they would be considered so if they beat their pupils? If your partner hit you, would it make you respect them?

Despite the claims of those who are pro-physical discipline, research that looked at the behaviour of 160,000 children sug-gests that physical punishment increases aggression, antisocial behaviour, cognitive difficulties and mental-health problems.[1] Not only does science indicate that physical punishment of children is very damaging, it also found that children who were smacked or spanked were more likely to defy their parents. In other words, it is ineffective and creates more problems. Speaking of the research findings Elizabeth Gershoff, Associate Professor at the University of Texas, stated that: 'Spanking was associated with unintended detrimental outcomes and was not associated with more immediate or long-term compliance, which are parents' intended outcomes when they discipline their children.'

The problem with rewards

Given that punishment is a poor regulator of child behaviour, one might assume that rewards would be a good alternative. After all, everybody likes to be rewarded. It makes us feel good. Surely making children feel good through rewards is the answer?

Ignoring the bad and rewarding the good forms the basis of many current parenting courses. Parents are taught to make a big fuss of the child, heap on the praise and offer rewards when they behave in a desirable way. A quick search of the internet reveals 726,000 entries for the term 'sticker chart' and 1,030,000 for 'reward chart'. Rewards are big business today. Stickers are commonly used in order to tame toddlers, stop tantrums, encourage children to eat meals, tidy their rooms and more. Most young children love stickers and, for the parent, they are seemingly not only effective, they are inexpensive too. Older children are often rewarded with special outings, games, sweets and, sometimes, money.

Rewarding good behaviour seems like a win–win, for both parent and child. The parents produce the desired behaviour in the child and the child feels good about their treat. Unfortunately, however, the positive effects are superficial. Scientific research indicates that this seemingly innocuous method of behavioural control may not provoke the desired learning response in our children. More concerning is that reward charts can actually negatively impact on the child's future behaviour. Research looking at toddlers found that those given a reward for a task were less likely to repeat it a second time without the offer of a reward, when compared to children who had not received a reward in the first place.[2] This suggests that the behaviours of young children are intrinsically motivated and are damaged when an extrinsic reward is offered. Rewards are a form of operant conditioning, in that they are reinforcers. They may temporarily control a child while they are on offer, but they do nothing to increase intrinsic motivation – remove the reward and the child no longer behaves in the way you wish.

Further research investigated the relationship between the use of rewards and the susceptibility of children to their negative effects.[3] Children and their parents were together, as a pair, assigned to either a control group (no reward offered) or one of four experimental groups (each of which involved a reward of some sort). The children were asked to help their parent with a task, which could be anything specified by the experimenter.

When this task was complete, the children were given an opportunity to help again, only this time no reward was on offer. The researchers found that those children who were rewarded worked well in the first task, but were far less likely to help in the second than those who had never received a reward. They also found that those children who were rewarded and whose mothers were positive about the reward helped more than those who received a reward but whose mothers were neutral or negative about it. From this, the researcher concluded that the effect of the reward may also be strongly tied to maternal actions and beliefs.

As most of the research shows, rewards can produce quick results, which is why they are so popular with the parenting experts you see on television. They walk into a house where tantrums and tears are the order of the day and seemingly turn around the behaviour of the children in under three days, often through offering rewards for 'good' behaviour. These immediate results make for good television, but what you don't see is what happens once the cameras stop rolling. After the initial quick improvement, it is quite likely the child will only behave well when rewards are on offer.

Rewards that increase extrinsic motivation temporarily can also have a very negative effect on intrinsic motivation. That means the more you reward your child for something, the less likely they are to repeat the behaviour. Or as author and educator Alfie Kohn[4] says: 'The more we want our children to want to do something, the more counterproductive it will be to reward them for doing it.'

No real learning takes place when children are disciplined using rewards; the child is simply complying because they want what is on offer. They are not learning right from wrong or becoming a better person. This is why so many parents who use reward charts have to keep using them, or resort to more and more extreme methods of what is effectively bribery to elicit the behaviour they want in their children. And while it may only be a sticker today, how do you get a thirteen-year-old to do what you ask of them? By using small rewards when the child is young, you are setting yourself up for greater issues when they are older.

I made the mistake of using a reward chart with my first-born. We ordered one with his favourite character, Thomas the Tank Engine, and stuck it proudly on the door of our refrigerator. We used big red removable spots and each time he behaved in a way that we desired we stuck a sticker onto the train tracks. The stickers were applied amid fanfares and applause and we explained why he had earned them. Temporarily, the stickers worked and his behaviour improved. After a while, we forgot about the reward chart. If we weren't at home, it seemed silly to add a sticker four hours later when we got home. If we went on holiday, we were without it and the two-week gap seemed to create a loss of interest. My son is a wonderful, charming, good-natured boy; however, he almost always has to be asked to do things several times and still frequently asks, 'What will you give me if I do it?' Perhaps this is unrelated to the sticker chart, but it seems too coincidental.

Using rewards with children ultimately results in 'If . . . then' behaviour, for example: 'If you let me go out with my friend, then I'll do my homework', or, 'If I eat my dinner, then will you give me some chocolate?' Each 'If . . . then' statement takes you into trickier territory and it becomes harder to repair the damage to your child's intrinsic motivation. If you would like to raise a child who wants to help people for no reason other than the fact they like to help people, or one who works hard at school simply because they enjoy bettering themselves, then you must avoid rewards whenever possible.

The negative effects of rewards are not just associated with children. The same applies to adults too. Recent research has found that something known as prosocial memory, or remembering to do something to help other people, is negatively affected by material rewards.[5] Researchers believe that the competition between self-gain on the one hand and helping others on the other leads to a problem with memory when it comes to prosocial behaviour. This makes sense if you consider the competing motives between self-gain (rewards) and altruism (helping others).

Distraction

If you ask parents how they cope with tantrums and difficult behaviour, more than 50 per cent will say that they often try to distract their child, so that they focus on something else. At first, this seems to be a good strategy. The child becomes calm, as does the parent, difficult situations are avoided and everyone is happier. Or are they?

Distraction can be one of the most damaging discipline tools if it is used too often. It prevents children from feeling, expressing and, therefore, managing emotions and, most importantly, it does not teach them anything useful for the future. Children learn socially acceptable behaviour and how to self-regulate by being allowed to express how they feel in a safe environment or, more, specifically, in the presence of somebody they love.

Imagine this scenario: you have just found out your partner is cheating on you. You have called your best friend in tears and they have arranged to meet up with you in the local park, so that they can comfort you. Now imagine the two of you sitting on a park bench. You start to tell your friend your story and, as you do so, your bottom lip starts to quiver and tears quickly follow. The more you say, the more you cry, until you are sobbing uncontrollably. Your friend may respond in one of two ways:

- **Response 1:** your friend puts their arm around you and gently says, 'It's OK. I'm here, let it out.' You cry a little harder and the tears continue to flow for another ten minutes, but at the end you feel a mild sense of relief. It feels good to let all of your big emotions out.

- **Response 2:** your friend loudly and very enthusiastically points towards the trees and says, 'Look, a squirrel! Can you see the squirrel running up the tree?' You look at your friend bemused as they then say, 'Look, an ice-cream van! Shall we go and get an ice cream?' You are so shocked that you stop crying as you begin to walk towards the ice-cream van together.

Which way would you want your friend to react? As nice as an ice cream may be, I'm guessing you'd go for Response 1. But why? Probably because it feels good to be listened to when we are sad or mad. It feels good to have somebody we love and trust supporting us with our feelings. It feels good to know that we're not in the situation alone. And, ultimately, when the tears stop, we feel better for the release. When we're distracted we are denied all of that.

Likewise, when you distract a child from their emotions you prevent them from discovering that emotions are OK. You deny them the chance to learn how to regulate their emotions and you take away the opportunity for them to learn how to handle a difficult situation alone. Perhaps most importantly, distraction encourages children to contain their emotions. Contained emotions can ultimately result in one of two responses: internalisation or externalisation. Research has found that just under 30 per cent of children experience internalising behaviour and 25 per cent experience externalising behaviour at some point in time.[6] This behaviour, or tendency towards it, is reduced, however, by a strong parental relationship. Internalising and externalising behaviours are known to increase as children enter adolescence.[7] Research has also shown that those who externalise during childhood are more likely to internalise during adolescence.[8] When a child internalises their big feelings – turning them inwards – it often results in low self-esteem, anxiety and depression and may also be related to eating disorders,[9] substance abuse, self-harm and suicide.[10] Externalising big feelings – projecting them out into the world – can result in aggression and violent behaviour, both physical and verbal. Allowing children to release their emotions as and when they happen can go a long way to reducing undesirable behaviour later.

Another problem with distraction is that the parents are prevented from learning better parenting skills. If a parent always distracts their children when potentially difficult situations arise, they never get a chance to practise more effective ways to discipline. This becomes problematic when children don't respond to distraction and alternative approaches are needed, and also when they are older and distraction no longer works at all, making parenting much harder.

I am often asked if there is ever a place for distraction. My response is always the same: yes, sometimes, but use it very sparingly and never make it one of your main parenting strategies. If you are at a funeral service with your child, for example, it makes sense to distract them, rather than allow them to express their feelings through shouting or crying. In these circumstances, distraction is perhaps the best option. But these occasions are rare. (See Chapter 14, where I explain my 70/30 rule: if you aim not to distract your child at least 70 per cent of the time, I think it is OK to do so the rest of the time when the situation demands a quick and quiet resolution to big feelings and difficult behaviour.)

Potentially gentle discipline methods

Not all mainstream discipline methods are negative and ineffective, you'll be pleased to hear. There are some approaches that, with a little tweaking, fit very well into the gentle-discipline ethos. Let's look at these.

Praise

Praise is very similar to rewards in terms of discipline. It can be considered a reinforcer when it comes to operant conditioning. It does not necessarily teach the child anything. If a child does something well, praise rewards them. If they do not please the parent, then the lack of praise begins to act like a punishment, or a punisher. If a child is used to receiving a great amount of praise, they may become more 'needy' for it and their self-esteem may become reliant on the opinions of other people. A child with self-esteem problems is usually a child who doesn't behave well.

Child psychologist Haim Ginott famously said: 'Praise, like penicillin, must not be administered haphazardly. There are rules and cautions that govern the handling of potent medicines – rules about timing and dosage, cautions about possible allergic reactions. There are similar regulations about the administration of emotional medicine.' [11] Used with care and caution, praise can be a useful discipline tool; however, most commonplace applications of praise are neither careful nor cautious.

Effective praise – that is, praise that has a positive effect on a child's behaviour, both in the short and long term – has the following features that differentiate it from ineffective or damaging praise:

Specific

Many parents will say 'Well done!' if a child shows them a painting that they have just completed. But what does this mean? At best, it is confusing for the child. What is it they have done well? Used nice colours? Painted neatly? Made a realistic picture? 'Well done' is meaningless, pointless and dismissive. It doesn't help children to learn, as it fails to tell them what it is that they have done that they should be proud of. If you like the way your child has drawn a cat in a picture, then tell them: 'I love your cat. It looks so happy!'

Effort-based and learning-focused

As I said earlier, if a child has been trying to tie their shoelaces for three months, yet you only congratulate and praise them when they finally manage it for the first time, you are over-looking all the previous hard work involved. Effort is so much more important than achievement. Praising effort and focusing on what the child has learned helps them to develop a growth mindset (see page 42): 'You've tried so hard to tie those laces today, what do you think you could change to make it easier?' Praising a child simply for achievement, on the other hand, develops a fixed mindset (see page 43). They learn that effort doesn't matter unless you achieve, and if you can't achieve, you may as well not put in the effort. Praising without reflection misses the potential for future growth. If a child does achieve, focus on how they can reflect on the success for future learning: 'You got an excellent score on that piece of work. What do you think you did really well this time?'

Changeable qualities

Children should only be praised for things that they have the power to change. 'You're so handsome', 'You're so clever' and 'My gorgeous girl' can all have potentially negative effects. The child is not able to change their looks or their innate intelligence, so praising them for qualities that are totally out of their control undermines them. What happens when they grow up and become unhappy with their looks, yet that is something you have praised them for constantly during their childhood. What happens when they struggle at school after you have been calling them clever for so long? At best, they won't believe you and, at worst, it may add to any disappointment or sense of failure that they feel.

Sportscasting

Sportscasting is exactly what it sounds like – commenting on your child's actions, rather like you might comment on a football match or Formula 1 race: 'Oh, Ben is building a really, really big tower . . . one, two, three – wow I can count it's ten blocks high'; or, 'Olivia is playing with the toy cars – I think she's about to race them . . . I wonder which one will win?' Sportscasting may feel strange at first, as it isn't an especially natural way of speaking. However, your child's reactions will make it well worth the effort and, in time, the technique feels much more natural.

Asking questions

Asking a child questions may not be direct praise, but it can really help them to feel validated and proud. If they are making models with bricks, ask them: 'What is that you're building? It looks fun.' Or, 'Why did you choose to make the house blue? Why did you choose to build a house?' The questions show your child that you are interested in what they are doing, and this interest helps to build their self-esteem, so that they think, My mum and dad care about what I do.

Appreciative or descriptive

With appreciative praise the child is given in-depth feedback from the parent about what they have done and why the parent appreciates it. This allows them to understand fully the praise and to assimilate it. Appreciative praise is descriptive, so rather than telling your child 'You're such a good girl', you describe clearly what has made you happy: 'I watched you pick up all of the toys and put them in the toy box; it's lovely and tidy in here now, isn't it? That will give us much more room to play a game together later.' This type of praise makes the child feel recognised and validated.

Praise is perhaps one of the hardest things to change when you begin to discipline in a gentle way. Most of us have been brought up with praise all our lives – whether from our parents, our teachers or a boss. Breaking this habit is hard, so cut yourself some slack. It's OK if you slip up and accidentally praise; just be aware of what you have said and vow to try to use more effective praise next time. With time it will come, but usually the first few months, even years, are hard. The key with using praise as a form of gentle discipline is remembering to keep it effort- not outcome-based, specific and descriptive.

Consequences

The dictionary definition of a consequence is: 'A result or effect, typically one that is unwelcome or unpleasant.' Consequences form a common part of discipline, particularly mainstream versions of it. The premise behind consequences, in most forms of discipline, is teaching children that their decisions and behaviour have results that are undesirable. Each time they do (or, indeed, don't do) something – usually related to a parental request – they are presumed to learn that the outcome of their behaviour is undesirable for them, the idea being that they then try to avoid the consequence by changing their behaviour. In many ways, consequences can be viewed as punishment. The reason for this is that there is a very fine line between effective consequences that teach children to do and be better and those which make them feel bad without necessarily teaching them anything, due to their inability to think critically, analytically and hypothetically (see page 58).

Used incorrectly, consequences can tip the balance of power towards parents. That may seem appealing, but it doesn't meet the description of a good and effective teacher. Remembering that a feeling of lacking control is a trigger for undesirable behaviour in children also helps us to understand why consequences may be an ineffective discipline tool that has the potential to make behaviour worse, not better. The key to using consequences gently is to consider the effect you are hoping to achieve and whether it is fair, age-appropriate and provides a good learning opportunity. In terms of being age-appropriate, as a general rule, the use of consequences is most suited to older children because of the cognitive skills needed to process them. If ever you are in doubt, it is better to avoid them.

Let's look at some of the most common consequences in use today and whether they can be viewed as gentle and effective and, indeed, whether there are better alternatives.

Illogical consequences

In many cases consequences are completely illogical. That is, there is no direct relationship between what the child has or hasn't done and what the parent is proposing as a consequence.

If the consequence is not clearly related to the child's behaviour, it can be confusing and can be viewed as punishment. This punishment is not likely to have the desired effect. Children punished with illogical consequences are likely to feel resentment towards their parents which, as we've seen, can cause a disconnect or a fragile connection. The fractured relationship between parent and child then tends to make the child's behaviour worse. If there is no clear and logical learning opportunity, the child will not change their behaviour on an internal or permanent basis and is likely to repeat the undesirable behaviour, or similar. Illogical consequences are judgemental and lack compassion and intuition.

Parents who use illogical consequences often find themselves in a battle of wills with their child. Often, they end up giving so many consequences – taking things away, banning certain activities and sending them to their room – that the child becomes almost immune, and might think, Well, I've lost everything I like, it doesn't matter what they do now. The undesirable behaviour may then continue and, in time, worsen.

Common examples of illogical consequences include the following:

- The child refuses to tidy their room, so they lose their pocket money for a week.

- The child refuses to do their homework, so the parent bans them from going to a friend's birthday party.

- The child hits another child at playgroup, so the parent says that they won't buy their weekly magazine in the supermarket the next day.

In each of the above cases, the consequence bears no relation to the behaviour. They really are just a punishment, from which the child does not learn in any true sense. And, for the most part, the parent is not trying to understand the motivation or reasons behind their child's behaviour. In effect, the child is simply punished for struggling with something. This has the potential to encourage them to internalise their feelings, leading to a greater degree of unease, which may possibly explode into something far bigger in the future.

Logical consequences

Logical consequences work with children, not against them. They are free of judgement and aid decision-making and learning. They work with a sense of mutual respect. Each logical consequence is a learning opportunity and helps children to make sense of how the world works. It is applied firmly but fairly and compassionately, its premise being sound and certainly gentle. The problem, however, is that many parents misuse them by applying them to children who are too young to understand them.

Logical consequences, by definition, rely on a child having a fairly good grasp of logical thought. They also require a degree of hypothetical thought. In Chapter 3 we learned that these cognitive skills are associated with the frontal lobe of the brain (see page 56) – the last section to fully mature. Children do not have a good degree of logical and hypothetical thought until they enter puberty. This doesn't mean that they lack these skills completely when they are younger, but they will be very immature. In order for logical consequences to be applied effectively, the child should be at least seven years old.

Logical consequences can work well with older children, particularly those approaching their teens. Ideally, the child will have an equal input in choosing them: ask them what they think should apply, or give them several to choose from. The more involvement the child has with the consequence, the better the learning opportunity will be. Preferably, the consequences will be agreed upon in advance with the child.

Here are some examples of logical consequences:

- Your child is listening to loud music in the living room, while you are attempting to make an important telephone call. You put the call on hold and calmly explain to them that you are struggling to hear the caller. You ask your child if they would prefer to turn the music right down while you are on the telephone or to turn it off and go into another room in order that they can play the music at the same volume.

  With this consequence you have made it clear that your child's current behaviour cannot continue – however, you have shown compassion for the fact that they are enjoying their music. You have given them two reasonable alternatives that consider both your needs. You have allowed the child to select an option that they prefer, giving them some autonomy. Finally, you have taught them to respect the needs of others and particularly that when somebody is having an important conversation that they need to be quiet.

- Your child comes home from school and tells you that they have lost their lunch box for the third time that month. You tell them that they will need to find something to take their lunch to school in. The options that they have are to find the lunch box, replace it with a new one using their own money or use an old lunch box or plastic tub until the old one is found or you have enough money to buy a new one.

  Here, you have shown compassion for your child, but you have also indicated that they need to take care of their possessions, as they are not always instantly replaceable. Your child hasn't been chastised, shouted at or punished, but you've made it very clear that you are not going to go straight out to buy a new lunch box and have given them options if they are not happy with this.

Here is an example of a logical consequence I used with my teenage son. My children are allowed one hour of screen time per day, which they usually choose to spend on a games console. On the whole, I can trust them to turn off the console at the end of their time, but sometimes I have to remind them if they are engrossed in a game. On one particular occasion, I was busy and forgot to remind my son to get off the console, although I suspect he did realise that his time was up. When I saw he had been on the console for around two hours I told him that he had gone over his time limit and that he had to get off immediately. He apologised and I asked him to think of a consequence that he was happy with. He replied, 'Well, if I don't have my hour tomorrow that makes up for the extra hour I had today.' He then remembered that he had a friend coming round the next day and that they had planned to play a match on the console. He got quite upset at this thought and asked if he could possibly miss his hour on the day after his friend's visit. I settled for this and, as agreed, he missed his turn two days later.

Here is an example of a logical consequence I used with my tween daughter. She is not one for keeping her room tidy, and every now and again we have to do a blitz in order to be able to see the floor again. I had asked her to tidy her room one Saturday morning and we had plans to go out for lunch on the same day. I reminded her that we needed to leave at twelve o'clock and that her room needed to be tidy by then. Half an hour before we were due to leave I checked on her and found her sitting on her bed reading a book, her room as messy as ever. I told her we only had half an hour to go and that if she wanted to come for lunch she had to hurry. At twelve o'clock I returned to the room to find she had done barely anything. At this point I told her that we wouldn't be able to go to lunch as her room was still a mess and now there was no time left to tidy it. She cried and I asked her if she would like me to help her. She nodded. We spent the next two hours tidying and once we had finished, I asked if she wanted me to make her something to eat, since she'd missed out on going out with me and hadn't yet eaten. Over lunch at home, we discussed the fact that we hadn't got to eat out together and how next week she was going to tidy as soon as I asked her, so that we could do it then instead.

Once you have decided on your consequences – preferably in partnership with your child – they should be applied consistently every time the behaviour happens. Effectively, logical consequences become the way you enforce boundaries with older children.

Natural consequences

Natural consequences happen, as their name suggests, as a natural result of something the child has – or has not – done. As such, they are not selected by the parent or the child. They are automatic, fast responses that carry an element of risk, and it is this risk, when it happens, that can help to shape the child's behaviour (although some natural consequences need to be repeated several times before they have an effect).

Here are some examples of natural consequences that may be appropriate for children over the age of three:

- Chasing a bee – could result in a sting.

- Touching a hot radiator – will hurt the hands.

- Playing with a bouncy ball close to a drain – the ball may be lost for ever.

- Not putting a coat on in cold weather – they might get a cold.

- A child who says something mean might be excluded by their friends.

- Not putting shoes on in the garden – they might step on a thorn.

- Playing with a cookie close to a paddling pool – it might fall in the water and be inedible.

- Putting a favourite electronic toy in the toilet – the toy will no longer work.

- Running too fast down a hill – they might fall over.

- Not keeping still when a cat is sitting on their lap – the cat might get down.

- Not putting up a hood or using an umbrella in the rain – they will get wet.

The following are natural consequences that are clearly too risky to allow with children:

- Putting hands into a fire – results in a burn.

- Running into the road – can result in being run over.

- Touching sharp knives – can result in being cut.

- Running at the edge of a swimming pool – they might fall in.

- Annoying a dog – they might get bitten.

Due to the risks involved, natural consequences need to be carefully considered in relation to the child's age. Generally, they are not suitable for children under the age of three, since they are unlikely to understand the consequence and may, therefore, be at much greater risk of something unpleasant happening to them as a result. Once they are three years old, however, natural consequences can be used to help them to learn, but only in situations where the risk is age-appropriate and safe.

Natural consequences must always happen immediately after the event. If they are delayed they are not natural. Also, they should only be allowed to happen if they directly involve the child and no one else. So, for example, if you are going out for the day and your child refuses to get dressed and you miss your train, this doesn't just affect them – all family members suffer.

One natural consequence that many parents seem to struggle with is the idea of children not eating. The natural consequence of a child refusing dinner would be that they go to bed hungry. If they don't want to eat their dinner because they're not hungry, that's OK. If they decide they are hungry an hour or two later, however, they shouldn't be denied food. Similarly, if a child doesn't eat dinner because they don't like the food on offer, they should not be denied other food. If an adult refuses a meal they still have the option to eat later, whether by cooking something else or paying for a takeaway. Children do not have this privilege. If my children refuse their dinner, I will ask them why. If the answer is that they are not hungry, I will offer to put the dinner in the microwave so that it can be heated up later. If they refuse to eat because they don't like what is on offer, then I'll suggest a quick and easy substitute. Our go-to alternatives are either breakfast cereal or toast with a topping. These are the only options, but they are always available should my children not want to eat what I have prepared, even if the food is something they have asked for. Withholding food from children is not an appropriate natural consequence – it is a punishment.

Positive consequences
Positive consequences happen when a child behaves in a desirable way and is rewarded by an unplanned natural outcome.

For instance, if you are tidying up after dinner and they help you without being asked, the task will take much less time and you might decide that there is time to go to the park before bedtime.

The use of positive consequences can reinforce and strengthen positive behaviour in children. Parents should be aware, however, that if the positive consequence is planned, it becomes a reward and rewards are fraught with many problems, as we have seen and will see again in the next chapter.

Consequences can be a useful discipline aid if used correctly and age appropriately. Used less mindfully, their effect can be the opposite to that desired. The following table summarises the different types of consequences:

Type of Consequence	Minimum Age Recommendation	Timing in Relation to Behaviour	What Is It?
Illogical consequences	Never	Often far too late	Punishment unrelated to the child's behaviour.
Logical consequences	Seven	No more than a few hours	An outcome directly related to the child's behaviour chosen by the parent and/or child.
Natural consequences	Three	Immediate	An automatic, natural outcome not chosen by parent or child.
Positive consequences	No minimum	Immediate	An automatic, positive outcome, not planned in advance. Not chosen by the child.

As we have discovered in this chapter, mainstream discipline is very often wide of the mark when we consider it from a mindful position. The techniques advocated are inappropriate in relation to the child's psychological abilities, and children are often punished with little thought as to the long-term consequences. Many of the methods have the potential to make behaviour *worse*, as they trigger difficult emotions in the children. Thinking back to the idea of teaching and learning and what we hope to show our children, we realise that many mainstream discipline methods set poor examples. With no role model to follow, no positive attributes to aspire to, their behaviour can often take a turn for the worse. The battle for control serves only to trigger the child, perhaps not immediately, but in the months and years to come.

That said, mainstream approaches are not all bad. It is possible to work with some of them, shaping them to fit you and your child, with a little forethought and understanding. (We have seen how praise and consequences can be used in a more effective and gentle manner, for example.) This is something I would like you to keep in mind as we move on to the next chapter about mainstream education.

Chapter 5

School Discipline

U nderstanding that punishment and rewards are poor ways to discipline children can leave many parents confused about the methods used in the classroom, where the focus has been on reward and punishment – or, rather, extrinsic motivation – for as long as schools have existed. We may no longer use the cane or a dunce hat, but, in most cases, school-based discipline is a matter of doing what has always been done with very little thought for anything outside this deeply entrenched system.

School discipline, particularly today when classrooms are overflowing and teacher recruitment and retention is falling, is largely centred on crowd control. In this discipline-for-the-masses approach, the individual needs of children tend to be overlooked. The emphasis is on control and compliance: the schools control; the children have to comply.

This observation is not meant as a criticism of teachers, or even individual schools. I know many teachers personally who subscribe to gentle discipline; indeed, they learned many of the same theories that I have covered in this book at university while training. Through my children's schooling I have come across many who are supportive, passionate, nurturing, inspiring and the very epitome of the 'good-teacher' role we have discussed here so much. I'm sure that if it was up to them, schools would look very different. Much of the problem stems from government demands, which take away the autonomy that teachers need in order to discipline effectively and to achieve the standards required of them. And schools often set behaviour policies that effectively inhibit teachers from working with their students in the way that they would like.

Even without unrealistic demands, teachers may struggle to control their class because of a few children whose behaviour is so poor that the time needed to discipline them means that their attention and focus are thinly spread across the rest of the class. Sometimes, these children come from homes where there is either no discipline or authoritarian discipline, where the child lives in a constant state of fear and rebellion. Other times, the children are living with undiagnosed special educational needs, such is the poor provision for support and diagnosis in most areas. Some children come to school with no coat, in dirty clothes and starving hungry and require the teacher to focus on them in order that their disadvantage is not so huge. With all this, on top of mountains of paperwork, lesson planning, homework marking and ever-increasing test preparation, it's no wonder that so many teachers are frustrated that they cannot teach as they would like. Make no mistake – in most cases the outdated, ineffective and non-gentle discipline used in schools today is not the fault of teachers.

But what are the implications for our children? We have worked our way into a position where the intrinsic motivation of students as young as four is damaged in order to control them in a broken and ever more tested system that doesn't meet any of their needs. It would take a large movement to steer us away from the current reward/punishment-based regime – one that, ironically, diminishes the individuality needed to begin this revolution.

For now, society remains deeply entrenched in the belief that children misbehave at school because they lack the motivation to do better. This belief leads policy-makers to use rewards to increase motivation to behave in ways that are seen as desirable, and punishment to decrease motivation to behave in ways that are seen as undesirable. This fundamental problem is discussed by author and education expert John Holt:

> This idea that children won't learn without outside rewards and penalties, or in the debased jargon of the behaviourists, 'positive and negative reinforcements,' usually becomes a self-fulfilling prophecy. If we treat children long enough as if that were true, they will come to believe it is true. So many people have said to me, 'If we didn't make children do things, they wouldn't do anything.' Even worse, they say, 'If I weren't made to do things, I wouldn't do anything.' It is the creed of a slave.[1]

While I do not mean to scaremonger, to focus purely on the positive would not be realistic or, indeed, particularly helpful. Parenting isn't all positive. It is full of ups and downs, highs and lows. If you are using, or plan to use, state education, discipline in schools is not an issue that can be glossed over. I believe that preparation and understanding are the keys to navigating this and in this chapter I will help you with both.

First, I want to look at the main problems with school discipline today. Importantly though, I will then discuss how you can help your child cope within the system and how you may even be able to change it. As I have said many times: you are your child's main teacher; never underestimate your own importance and the effect you can have on your child over and above any other teacher.

School discipline: the problems

Let's look at the top incorrect assumptions and applications of discipline that you may – or perhaps already have – come across at school.

The mistaken belief of motivation

If a child misbehaves at school, the almost universal assumption is that the child is lacking in motivation to do better. If a child fails to complete their homework, or doesn't focus during lessons, gossiping with friends instead, it is often presumed, again, that they need to be motivated to do better. Commonly, the child will end up covered in stickers saying, 'I listened well today', or, 'I did good work today'; or they will come home clutching achievement certificates or be rewarded with house or class points that can be traded in for a treat.

If a child is disruptive in class, loses their temper quickly or is verbally or physically violent, it is, again, often presumed that they need to be motivated to do better. They might be kept in at playtime, sent to after-school detention or even isolated or suspended.

In all cases, the school completely misses the real issue and effectively punishes the child for having a problem. Although rewards may not seem like punishment, they are if they remain beyond a child's reach. They might as well be told: 'You didn't do well enough today, so you don't get anything nice.' Focusing on motivation, as we've seen previously (see pages 53 and 76) is the wrong route to take, for the problem is more likely to be about ability.

Rewarding or punishing children for a certain behaviour assumes that they have the ability to change it. Aside from requiring a large degree of logical and hypothetical thinking that may not be present at a younger age (see page 58), the idea that a child is simply demotivated to change and that dangling a carrot or a stick will provide the necessary incentive is wrong. Most undesirable behaviour at school is caused by children experiencing difficulties – perhaps relating to friends, home, something of a sensory nature, concentration or a lack of understanding. How do rewards and punishments fix these problems? They don't. In fact, they are likely to make the child feel even worse, by highlighting the fact that they do not have the skills needed to change their behaviour. This, in turn, damages their self-esteem and any pre-existing intrinsic motivation.

In the case of a child who doesn't concentrate at school – say, they constantly move around or chatter during lessons or perhaps they gaze off into the distance daydreaming – most schools would send the child out of the class for being disruptive, perhaps asking the parents to come in and speak to the headteacher, putting the child on report or enrolling them in a scheme where a reward is offered for improved behaviour. Every one of these approaches starts with the assumption that the child knows how to and, indeed, *can* change their behaviour. And if they cannot, then they are punished. The proper action here would be to look for the root cause of the behaviour. *Why* is the child not concentrating? Are they tired? Can they see and hear properly? Is the teacher not taking account of different learning styles? Is the child being expected to sit still for too long? Would they benefit from regular breaks and being allowed to move around or an object to fiddle with? Are they understanding what is being said in lessons? Would they benefit from some extra catch-up tuition, so that they are on the same level as their peers? How do they feel about school? Are they confident or are they struggling with something? Is there a possibility that the child has a learning disorder or disability? When schools ask these questions they can go on to think about how they can provide bespoke support. When children are treated as individuals and helped to behave in more acceptable ways, that's when change really happens. Parents should be asking their child's school, 'Why is my child behaving like this?' – before the school jumps in with, 'How we are going to motivate this child to behave better?'

In the case of a child who is violent, or one who bullies others, the school should ask, 'Why?' Why is the child behaving in this way? What has caused them to feel so uncomfortable? Are they being bullied themselves? (Bullying others is often a strong sign that a child is being bullied.) Are they struggling to control their temper? Are they lacking in emotion regulation and intelligence skills? Asking these questions is acknowledging that the child is somehow suffering and it helps to solve their problems. Motivating them through punishment and rewards does not change their suffering – it just adds to it, effectively penalising them for having a problem.

Labelling children and fixed mindsets

Perhaps one of the most damaging effects of common school-discipline principles is on children's self-belief and self-esteem. Ironically, many schools talk of teaching children to have a growth mindset, yet their behaviour policies foster a fixed one. The more children are punished for their behaviour (via rewards as well), the greater the chance that they will develop a fixed mindset. If the child is incapable of changing their behaviour because of a lack of ability, then they will quickly come to believe that they are whatever people say about them – that this is who they are. Children can easily be labelled as naughty, difficult, disruptive or violent, even if these words are never spoken by teachers. A child who is constantly suffering for their behaviour and being treated differently from their peers because they lack the ability to change will soon think that it is not worth trying.

Again, taking time to uncover the root cause of the child's behaviour and working with them, rather than using rewards and punishments, helps them to know that somebody is on their side. Right now, they do not have the ability to change alone, but in the future they will, thanks to somebody who believes in them. This hope does wonders for their self-esteem, and considering that many 'misbehaviours' happen when a child is feeling bad, just knowing that they are getting help can be a catalyst for improvement, while the new skills develop.

Let's look at some of the most common school discipline methods, and their problems, in a little more detail. As you read through them, ask yourself how they help the child to change their behaviour and what sort of a mindset they foster.

Missing breaks and playtime

Missing break time features strongly in school-discipline methods. Younger children may be kept in to speak to the teacher, catch up on work that they missed during class because they weren't concentrating or finish homework that wasn't given in. Sometimes, they miss break simply because the teacher uses it as a punishment. Older children who are approaching their teens will be given the same sanction, only now it is called a lunchtime detention. Detentions may be given for all manner of things, from bad behaviour to missing homework.

How do you think the child feels when their friends are enjoying break time – playing, chatting or even eating – and they are inside a classroom with a teacher. What effect do you think the exclusion has upon them? Does it help them to learn a better way or new skills? What if the child is in trouble for messing around in class and not concentrating? Here the missed break is completely at odds with what the child needs most – to move freely outdoors. The punishment is entirely illogical.

Class and school exclusions

When children are young, they may be sent outside the classroom if they misbehave. Sometimes, they are sent to sit in a corridor, in a corner of the room alone or in the headteacher's office. When they are older they are sent to isolation rooms or temporarily excluded from the school. Understandably, teachers have a duty to protect all children in their class. They also have a responsibility to provide the best education they can to all of their students. Neither of these is possible with a constantly disruptive child.

Although it would appear to make sense to remove the troublesome child from the class in order to protect the others, there is an assumption here that the excluded child will learn from their punishment. But how does separating a child from their class and their peers help them to resolve the underlying problem that is causing their behaviour? How does it make them feel? Does it motivate them to do better and, indeed, believe that they *can* do better or not?

Unfortunately, removal from the class or school doesn't improve behaviour and may make it worse.[2] It is especially damaging if the child is already finding it hard to fit in or to be understood, and exclusion, in any form, often increases the disconnect between a child and the education system. Research has shown that taking disruptive children out of a class doesn't just negatively affect them, but makes their friends and the whole of their network feel unsettled too.[3]

School reward systems

School rewards tend to be incredibly superficial and go against all of the rules we know about effective praise. They almost always focus on outcome and not effort, despite claims that they aim to produce growth mindsets.

Achievement certificates and awards are great examples of outcome-based praise. Warnings of lost golden time, behaviour ladders, sad and happy clouds and traffic lights are all systems focusing on visual representations of behaviour consequences, which can leave children who are unable to behave better feeling excluded from their peers and also shamed for being on the lower 'bad' levels. These feelings are heightened if the rewards aimed for are class-based – for instance, a class party or treat – and they add to the lack of intrinsic motivation caused by rewards.

How do you think children who are struggling with their behaviour feel when they fail to achieve a reward? Or if their behaviour costs their classmates a treat? And if a child does receive a reward, do you think it will motivate them to get another, even though research says the opposite? How do rewards help children, struggling over the skills or abilities that they lack, to behave in a way that is acceptable to the school?

How could schools change?

When I speak about school discipline, I am often asked: 'So what would *you* do, then?' Many involved in education say that it is very difficult to do it any other way. And I agree. Working with too little support, too many demands from governments, with a lack of teachers and too many children is hard. But it's not impossible. The real question is: do those involved in education have the confidence to change and the desire and effort required to do what is needed?

I don't have a magic solution. There is no simple answer. However, there are several elements which, when brought together consistently, could spell out a really effective form of discipline, aligned with a great education.

Steps to improve school discipline

1   **Training** All teachers should aim to work with the qualities of the 'good teacher' outlined in the Introduction to this book. Improving these skills may require teachers to have more training in child psychology and neuroscience, so that they have a good knowledge of how the brain develops at each age and which cognitive skills children are capable of at any given time. In addition, they should have training in effective communication strategies and self-regulation of their own emotions. These should all be in addition to their initial teacher training and continue indefinitely while in practice.

2   **Connections** Teachers should try to form good connections with all of their pupils. This is the best way to reduce unwanted behaviour and increase intrinsic motivation in children. If children genuinely love being in their teacher's presence, they will want to please them and work well for them. If the teacher–student connection is good, then the teacher will notice when all is not right in a child's world and help them before problems escalate. A good connection allows children to speak to their teachers about what is wrong, rather than showing it through their behaviour. Mutual respect is also a key

goal. When teachers respect their students, their students are, in turn, more likely to respect them.

3 **Breaks** Children of all ages should have regular breaks – ideally, at least once an hour. These breaks need not be long; just five minutes outside usual break times in the playground and lunch can make a huge difference. Regular breaks can aid concentration, especially if the children are encouraged to move around.

4 **Individuality** Schools should provide plenty of opportunities for children to express their individuality. All children can excel at something, but few excel at everything. Finding each child's niche is important for raising self-esteem. Giving them the chance to learn a wide variety of subjects and skills allows them to feel proficient at and excited by something, which helps to raise their intrinsic motivation to learn.

5 **Identifying problems** If a child is struggling and misbehaving it is really important to find out what ability or skill they are missing. When it has been identified, working with the child, whether one-to-one or in a small group – to improve or gain that skill or ability is important. And once it has been learned, the unwanted behaviour naturally diminishes.

6 **Autonomy** Children have very little control over their learning at school, no matter how old they are. Increasing their autonomy and allowing them to lead their own learning whenever possible can have a very positive effect. In addition, inviting children to make democratic choices as part of a class or peer group can give them a greater sense of belonging and self-esteem.

7   **Communication** A strong relationship with parents is vital for all schools and teachers. Regular, open and transparent communication is important. This shouldn't just happen during parents' evenings, and it needs to be fostered by both parties. Teachers should feel supported by parents, but equally, they must support and listen to parents and problem-solve collaboratively.

8   **Fresh air** No matter how old they are, children need to get outside more and learn from nature. Being outside and being able to move more freely helps with concentration, motivation and self-esteem. Classroom-based learning, at any age, is in direct conflict with what children need.

9   **Less testing** The constant threat of tests can have a terrible effect on children. If tests have to take place, then they should be executed in as calm and stress-free manner as possible, with no cramming or endless past papers. If the tests are a measure of the school, and not important to the children's future, then children and their parents should be made aware of this and there should, accordingly, be no pressure to perform.

10   **Less homework** Homework largely serves to take away important free time from children when they should be relaxing and it has no positive impact on their education. If homework is set, it should be fun and child-led, whatever the age. Instead of worksheets and photocopied question papers, children should be set projects and investigative work that they can enjoy.

11   **School age** The school starting age should be raised – preferably to seven, in line with much of Scandinavia where, incidentally, some of the best educational outcomes in the world are reported. If not, however, then

it should be raised at least to five years old, especially if the child is summer born. A child starting school when they have just turned four is not in line with their developmental needs.

12 **The school day** School should start later in the day for teenagers. As children enter puberty, their body clocks go through a strange temporal shift. Biologically, they need a much later bedtime. They become natural night owls. As a result, they also need a later wake-up time, which the early start at school precludes. Research shows that mean bedtime during adolescence is 10.30 p.m.[4] The recommended sleep duration for this age is ten hours. Therefore, it is not natural for teenagers to wake until 8.30 a.m. A more appropriate school start time with this in mind would be 9–9.30 a.m.

What happens when discipline at school and at home are different?

Whenever I run gentle-discipline workshops, I am always asked: 'Can you ever mix mainstream school and gentle parenting? Doesn't the discipline used at school undo all of the good work that you do at home?' Children spend far more time at home with their parents than they do at school. They sleep for an average of eleven hours per night, which means they spend ninety-one hours per week awake. With an average school day of six hours and fifteen minutes, that means they are at school for around thirty-one hours – just 34 per cent of their waking time. And this doesn't even take school holidays into account. You, therefore, have the most impact on their behaviour by far. So yes, it is possible to mix the two.

It may be that nothing I have included in this chapter resonates for some of you. There are some genuinely wonderful schools and teachers, and perhaps you have been lucky enough to find them. If your school does fit very much within the descriptions in this chapter though, don't despair, as there are ways that you can effect change.

The first step should always be to speak to your child's teacher about any discipline issues. If this doesn't prove fruitful, then a meeting with the head of year or headteacher is next on your list. Most schools have their behaviour policies on their website for you to download; if yours doesn't, request a copy in advance of your meeting. (Incidentally, if you have yet to select a school for your child, always start with their behaviour policy.) Go into any meeting with teachers with realistic expectations – you will not be able to change everything, but you could, for instance, achieve an initial goal such as stopping your child being kept in at break time. Prioritising your concerns is the way to go. You might also consider joining the board of parent governors to increase your say in the way things are run, and even have an input into staff recruitment.

Speaking with the school isn't your only job. You must also speak to your child. It's OK for you to pursue your own methods of discipline at home, but you need to explain to your child why they are expected to behave differently at school. Most children can understand from the outset that they may get stickers or certificates at school, but these are not things that happen at home. Help them to appreciate that you have chosen for them to attend their school and therefore you have to be respectful of the rules, even though you don't agree with them. These conversations, and the support that you give at home, can really help your child to be more accepting of school discipline. In some ways, this is wonderful preparation for life for your child, especially for the world of work.

Why children behave differently at home and at school

Have you ever noticed that your child's behaviour is dramatically different at school and at home? Perhaps they behave like an angel at school, but you really struggle with them at home? Or maybe they struggle at school, but you don't have any issues at home?

If you don't experience the same sort of behaviour that your child's teachers report, then the chances are it is the school causing the problem – be it people, environment or expectations. If you find yourself in this situation, it is important that, together with the school, you find what is triggering your child and resolve it.

If you find your child is behaving badly at home, and yet the school say that they are perfectly behaved, then once again it is highly likely that the problem lies at school. Why is this? Quite simply, your child has been putting on an act all day. They have been 'behaving well' and doing what is expected of them at school. It is a pretty tough act though, and while many children can do a great job of keeping up the façade all day, when they get home the mask drops. It's almost as if they're saying, 'Oh, thank goodness. I can stop pretending now. I can be me now I'm home with people who love me.'

A child who has been struggling at school will often pour out their frustration, anger and sadness once they are home. They feel safe with you. They know they can be whoever they want to be because you love them unconditionally. They can finally offload. Out come the tears and the anger that they have held in all day and the sheer frustration that they have hidden. It is not that you've done anything wrong. It is simply that they finally feel able to be their authentic self with you – precisely because you've done everything right! This behaviour can be difficult to cope with as a parent, particularly if you are also in need of 'releasing' yourself after a long and tough day. It is, however, the biggest compliment your child could pay you. When they have a meltdown they are saying, 'I love you. I feel safe with you. Thank you for letting me be myself.' Try to remind yourself of this the next time it happens. Allow the emotions to flow. Don't try to stop them. It's a good thing.

Ultimately, there is a good chance that your child will attend a school with very different behaviour expectations and discipline methods from those you use at home. But as long as they are well supported by you, they are actually far more adaptable than you think, no matter how undesirable the fall-out behaviour may be. Remember that there may be elements of your school's discipline policy that you can change, either via conversations with staff or by joining the board of governors, if you feel strongly. If your child is really struggling at school or you have yet to enter the system and you are not sure if it is for you, there are many options available, from state-run free and democratic schools to private Steiner and Waldorf alternative schools to home-educating or unschooling (home educating with no specific syllabus or lessons).

The most important point to focus on is that it is their time with you that matters. Even before they start school, your child will have at least four years at home with you – that's a long time to embed gentle-discipline practices and create a resilient child with the confidence and independence to thrive in almost any situation.

Chapter 6

Coping with Violent and Destructive Behaviour

This chapter, along with Chapters 7 to 13, will concentrate on applying what we have learned up till now to specific behaviour scenarios. If you are struggling with a particular issue, you can now skip to the relevant chapter for immediate help. For a complete understanding, however, do come back and read all of the other chapters. While they may have a certain focus, the information contained in them is still valuable.

Of all the behaviour challenges parents struggle with, violent behaviour has to be the hardest. A child who hits, kicks or bites can test the patience of even the calmest parent. When a child is violent, it can seem that they are deliberately trying to hurt you or others and it can be very easy to take it personally. Many parents worry that the child will remain violent and grow up into an antisocial adult who will constantly get in trouble. Others wonder what on earth they did wrong to create such violence.

Why are children violent?

In most cases, violent behaviour in children is not a reflection of their parenting, but rather of immature emotion regulation and difficulty adjusting in a certain environment or place in the family. It often happens when a child feels vulnerable, anxious or out of control. They don't mean to be violent – they simply cannot control their reactions. In all cases they are stuck in a fight-or-flight response, whereby something triggers them, causing psychological upset, and their body – or, more specifically, their sympathetic nervous system – responds as if their life was under threat. At this moment in time survival is key. The body is flooded with catecholamines (stress hormones), including adrenaline. It also secretes hormones including cortisol. These all serve to put the body on high alert: heart rate and blood pressure are raised, blood flow to skeletal muscles is increased and the body is readied for action (fighting or running).

We have all experienced this response and know how it feels to be so 'on edge' and ready to explode. This is the state violent children find themselves in on an almost daily basis. The difference is that, as adults, we have the brain development necessary to control our responses. If we become very scared or very angry, although we may feel desperate to hit something, we know it is not socially acceptable and we can usually restrain ourselves. We can talk ourselves down, take some deep breaths and respond in an appropriate way. Children do not have the same ability; they are often violent because they can't do better.

So what triggers this reaction in violent children? The causes are as unique as the child. Each will have their own personal triggers. There are, however, some common causes:

Feeling overwhelmed

If a child feels overwhelmed in a certain situation, it will put them on high alert. For toddlers, this can include toddler groups, full of noise and busyness. For preschoolers, it could be another child invading their body space. For school-aged children, it could be the pressures of being at school. The transition of starting school or nursery for the first time can be a huge trigger for children. Similarly, the transition to secondary school can be another one. Children can struggle to adjust to the environments, routines and expectations. And if they are unable to cope with overwhelming feelings, they may enter a fight-or-flight state, which can result in violent behaviour.

Feeling disconnected

If a child feels disconnected from their teachers, peers, friends or, in particular, parents, they may be more prone to violent behaviour. This is heightened if they are desperate for more one-to-one attention from a loved one. Anything that causes a disconnect, such as a mother returning to work, a child starting day care or the arrival of a new sibling can leave them feeling vulnerable and a fight-or-flight response may occur as a result. Needing more attention is not a bad thing, as so many incorrectly believe. Children need our attention as much as they need air to breathe. If they do not get enough of it and feel disconnected, we often see the results in their behaviour.

Being bullied

A child who hits, kicks or bites other children is commonly perceived to be a bully. But what many parents don't realise about bullying is that it is often a sign that the child is being bullied themselves. In a way, the bullying allows them to regain a sense of control. If your child is at school and appears to be bullying others, always investigate whether they themselves are being picked on.

Modelling behaviour

Children are great mimics. In Chapter 1 we looked at Albert Bandura's theory of Social Modelling and how this effect impacts on all behaviour. No matter how your child is behaving you should always ask yourself: 'Have they picked this up from me or somebody else in their life?' This is why it is so important to discipline in a calm and respectful way at all times. How you behave towards your child is how they will behave towards others.

In this case, however, it may not necessarily be people who are causing the behaviour. If your child is acting violently, they may be modelling something they have seen on television, in computer games, in a book, at nursery or school or, indeed, the behaviour of their peers.

How to encourage more appropriate behaviour

How can you change the behaviour of a violent child? I like to answer this in three words. Why? How? What? This is a framework I use to help decide upon the most gentle and effective discipline approach to different issues. I will use it throughout the following chapters.

- Why is the child behaving this way? Has something triggered the behaviour? Is it developmentally normal?

- How is the child feeling? Are they acting this way because they are feeling bad?

- What do you hope to teach the child when you discipline them?

Let's start with the 'Why?' Why is the child acting this way? Can you find the root cause? Are they feeling overwhelmed? Are they needing to reconnect? Are they lacking autonomy? Are they being bullied? Are they lacking the communication skills necessary to express themselves in words? Are they modelling the behaviour of someone else? Can you remove them from the triggers of their behaviour? Are they simply behaving in an age-appropriate way and lacking self-regulation skills?

Next, let's look at how the child is feeling. Are they scared? Are they feeling that you no longer love them, or don't love them as much as their sibling or your new partner? Are they afraid that you will leave them? Are they desperately crying out for your help and attention? Are they feeling sad and left out by their peers at school? Are they feeling inadequate and lacking in confidence and self-esteem at school? There is always an underlying feeling accompanying violent behaviour.

Lastly, think about what you hope to achieve from a discipline perspective. Do you simply want to stop the undesirable behaviour, or do you want to fix the child's problems and help them to manage their emotions? Asking yourself these questions will direct the discipline you choose. Taking 'time in' with the child can help them to learn more appropriate behaviour and also help them to feel supported. Working on coping skills and strategies can help them to feel better and improve their behaviour. Non-gentle discipline, such as time out, naughty steps, grounding and removing privileges, such as pocket money, doesn't help to teach the child the skills they lack. If you want to change the behaviour, help them feel better and teach more appropriate behaviour, you always have to consider why they are behaving as they are and also how they feel. These two together will tell you what to do.

In terms of appropriate discipline, you should always start with safety: that of your child, yourself, others and objects around you. Usually, this means moving the child away from potential harm and the potential to harm others. Once you, your child and others are safe, you can work on how to respond. There are two options: the first is an in-the-moment response and the second is the long-term response.

When thinking in the moment, you need to think about how to cease the behaviour as quickly as possible in a way that is considerate and supportive. Calmly and firmly tell your child that their behaviour is not acceptable. Keep it as short and concise as possible. When they are in fight-or-flight mode they will not listen to reasoning and lengthy explanations. A simple 'I will not let you do that' is enough for now; explanations come later, when the child is calmer. There may be instances when you need to move the child away or hold them in a way that they cannot harm themselves or others; however, any moving or holding should be as gentle and respectful as possible. Tell them what you are doing, but always give them the opportunity to do it themselves first. Now is the time to sit with them and support them. Offer to cuddle them or just sit close and listen, if they do not want to be touched. Allow them to cry as much as they need to and make it clear that it's OK. Once they are calm, it's time to explain why what they did was wrong and speak about alternative ways they could behave. Remember that you are teaching them and there is no place for your own anger or chastisement here.

From a long-term perspective, when the child is calm, you can, as a team, work out ways in which they can manage their emotions in a way that doesn't harm other people. Highlight that it is OK for them to be angry, but that they must handle their anger in a more effective way. Don't tell them not to get so angry all the time; they cannot control how they feel and there is nothing wrong with being angry. Instead, help them to learn to manage their feelings better. There are several good books on the market about this (see Resources, page 266), but here are a few tips that can help:

- Carrying a stress ball in their pocket at all times

- Counting to ten slowly in their heads before responding

- Picturing themselves in a favourite spot, perhaps on holiday, and using it to feel happy

- Imagining what the other person will feel if they hurt them

- Imagining an 'anger dial' in their mind and turning it down from high (red), to low (blue)

- Pretending to blow out candles on a birthday cake

- Pinging a rubber band on their wrist

- Closing their eyes, scrunching up their face really tightly and then letting it relax

- Giving their anger a funny name and then telling him or her to 'please go away' when they appear

- Asking you for help as soon as they feel themselves getting angry

- Repeating 'I am calm' ten times in their mind.

Your child could also think of their own coping technique. If they are young, you could read or make up a story about a violent child and then ask your child if they can think of ways to help. You could role-play alternatives with them or ask them to draw a mind map if they are older. You could even ask them for their advice for yourself!

Frequently asked questions about violence in children

There are four questions I am commonly asked when it comes to childhood violence. I'd like to answer these in a fairly specific way to give you some pointers, but what I can't tell you is how to consider the 'Why? How? What?' for your unique situation. So the answers below should be used alongside your understanding of why your own child is behaving in this way, how they are feeling and what, specifically, you hope to gain from disciplining them.

How can you stop a child biting others?

If a baby bites you, it is likely to be due to one of three things. First, biting is common when a baby is teething and the pain in their gums is relieved by biting something quite firmly. Second, a baby tends to explore everything with their mouth because it is such a sensory place, and biting down on flesh may feel good to them. Lastly, they may bite as an expression of affection. While this may seem to be anything but affectionate, to some babies it is an expression of how much they love you. Have you ever told your child, 'I love you so much, I could just eat you up'? That's exactly what some biting babies do.

If your baby bites you, gently but quickly put them down; delatch them, if you are breastfeeding, or move them away from you while saying, 'Oww, biting hurts.' If your baby cries after this, which most will, pick them up and comfort them and say, 'It's OK, I love you', but if they do the same again, repeat the words and actions. From a gentle-discipline perspective, it would be much nicer to be able to say, 'Gentle with your teeth', and while this is a good response for toddlers, it is too complex for babies. Most will simply just look at you and smile or giggle. You also need to fulfil their need to bite, and teething jewellery works very well for this, particularly if you are wearing it and redirect the baby every time they bite, or look like they are about to do so. As you redirect, say, 'I won't let you bite me, but you can bite this.' You can expect to have to repeat this many times before your baby catches on, but if you are consistent, ultimately they will.

Toddlers or preschoolers who bite are usually indicating some form of psychological distress. The most common reasons for biting in this age group include a need for more attention from you, especially if they have just become a big brother or sister. They may direct their biting at you or at their new sibling. Either way, the cause is the same. They are saying, 'Please love me as much as you did before. I'm hurting. I need your attention.' Biting in this age group can also be a child's response to feeling overwhelmed or unable to cope with their personal space being invaded. This happens a lot at nursery and playgroup. The child is saying, 'I can't take this any more. Please give me the toy and leave me alone.' In this instance, biting is a stress response and a protection mechanism to reduce stress levels. Lastly, children in this age group may bite out of frustration at you. If you ask them to do – or, indeed, stop doing – something, they may bite as a way of saying, 'Please don't ask me to do that. I don't want to. I can't cope.'

Understanding the cause is obviously important. If you remove the trigger, you will rapidly diminish the biting. In the meantime, when the child bites you or somebody else, loudly and firmly say, 'Stop – I won't let you bite', and move the child out of biting distance. At this point, do not go into a lengthy explanation of why biting is bad. The child is not in the right state to listen to logic and reason. Keep it short and clear. Once you have moved them, repeat the phrase, 'I won't let you bite', and be prepared to comfort them when they inevitably cry. Once they are calm, you can explain why they shouldn't bite and, lastly, what they should do instead. As with babies, biting in young children can take some time to 'fix' due to their immature brain development. The chances are that they will bite again and, when they do, repeat the same process. In time, hopefully, you can reduce the triggers and condition a different response that does not involve biting.

How can you stop a child hitting or kicking others?

Kicking in children is usually an anger or fear reflex. Something triggers them to enter fight-or-flight mode and the chemicals flooding their body prompt them to hit or kick – to 'fight', rather than run away. When children are in this state, there is no point trying to talk them out of their behaviour. The state of high alert that they are in will inhibit their ability to listen to you and rationalise their behaviour. Your role at this point is to remove your child from the person they are hurting. Removing them not only helps to keep the other party safe, but also helps your child by distancing them from the trigger. At this point, firmly state: 'I will not let you kick/hit.' Stay with the child while they cry, shout or squirm and repeat again: 'I will not let you kick/hit.' Once they have calmed down, you can explain to them why their behaviour is unacceptable and what they can do instead. It is important to understand that it is OK for them to be angry; your aim is not to stop them getting angry, but to help them release their anger in a more acceptable way. When they are calm, talk with them about what happened. Ask how they were feeling and brainstorm some ways that they can diffuse their anger without hurting others next time.

If the child has hit or kicked you because they did not like what you asked them to do, the same process is applicable, but once the child is calm, discuss alternatives to your request. For instance, if they have hit or kicked you because they have refused to tidy something away, you might suggest that you help them, or that they can tidy half now and half after a snack. It is important that you don't drop your initial request due to their behaviour. Stop the violent behaviour, sit with the child while they cry and then return to your request.

If the child is hitting or kicking at day care or school, your first step should be a meeting with their key worker or teacher. While you can discuss alternative ways to react at home and arm your child with a list of coping mechanisms, you cannot control what happens at school or day care, or how the adults there respond. First, you need to find out what triggered the behaviour and how school or day care can help your child to navigate a similar situation next time, or to reduce the possibility of it happening again. Next, you should agree with day care or school how they will respond the next time the behaviour happens because it almost certainly will. You should agree on a response that is similar to the way you would handle the situation at home – for instance, removing the child from the situation and sitting with them until they are calm, before discussing what happened. Lastly, you should share the coping mechanisms you have discussed at home with your child's key workers or teachers and ask them to employ similar methods when they see your child struggling. Communication and consistency between home and a day care or school setting is vital. You have to be prepared to work together to solve the problem. Far too many settings expect the parent to resolve the problem with little input from them. Sadly, this is very unlikely to work and just highlights the fact that day care or school are part of the problem.

How can you stop a child kicking or punching objects?

Children who kick and punch objects are most likely feeling very similar to those who kick or punch people. In many ways, violence towards objects is better than that towards people as no one is hurt. However, it can cause more problems if the child breaks precious objects, those belonging to other people or even in a shop. Finding and working with the triggers is, once again, key. In addition, accepting the child's emotions but helping them to diffuse them in a more suitable way is the ultimate goal. In the moment, however, your main focus should be on reducing the damage caused, by moving your child, or the target of their anger, away. Firmly say, 'I will not let you kick/punch that', and support them to release their feelings by moving away with them to a safe and quiet area. When they are calm, discuss why what they did was not appropriate and better ways that they could express their emotions.

For tweens and teens, you can also use logical consequences in the form of asking them to replace damaged objects with pocket money or earnings from weekend jobs, as applicable.

How can you stop a child throwing objects?

Young children who throw objects may not always be doing so out of anger. In fact, it is more likely that they are throwing because of a developmental stage that they are in. Children going through a trajectory schema (see page 51) will often throw anything they can because they are learning about the movement of objects. This throwing practice tells them about basic rules, such as gravity and speed. A toddler or preschooler who throws inappropriate objects probably needs more physical entertainment. When you see them about to throw something, say: 'Stop! Hold on to that please.' By telling them what you want them to do, rather than shouting, 'No, don't throw', you are making it far more likely that they will listen and respond because you are focusing on the positive, rather than a vague or negative instruction. You should also give them as much opportunity as possible to throw safe objects, such bean bags or balls in the garden. If possible, after you have stopped the child from throwing, follow up with a safe suggestion: 'You can't throw the ornament, but we can go outside and throw your ball if you want?'

Older children who throw things when they are angry should be treated in exactly the same way as when they kick or punch objects. Firmly tell them to stop what they are doing, support them afterwards and, when they are calm, explain the consequences of their actions.

Real family case studies

The remainder of this chapter is devoted to real correspondence between myself and parents who have struggled with violent behaviour in their children. While these questions relate to children of a specific age, my answers can be universally applied. As you read through them, see if you can identify the cause of the behaviour (the 'Why?'), an understanding of how the child feels (the 'How?') and what a good discipline solution would be (the 'What?').

Q: *Our son is four. His little sister was born six months ago. Since her arrival I have carried her in a sling, breastfed her and bedshared with her and have hardly put her down. She is a wonderful little girl and very, very happy. Everyone comments on how happy she is. Her brother, on the other hand, is not so happy. He hits me and his sister. I try to ignore this, but find it hard not to close doors on him in order to keep the baby safe. He also throws things. He is very strong and can easily hurt both of us. He spits and says, 'Ha, I've just spat on the floor!' I just say, 'That's not very nice, but if you want to do it, then do it.' This morning I asked him whether he wanted to come upstairs with me to get his school clothes, or if he wanted me to get them and bring them downstairs myself. He chose for me to get them and bring them down. When I got upstairs he started crying and saying that I'd left him downstairs. I explained that I'd given him a choice, but told him to just come upstairs and I'd wait at the top of the stairs. He said, 'No, come and get me', to which I replied, 'No, I will wait at the top of the stairs.' He then cried and had a meltdown. Something similar happens daily. Yesterday it was him wanting help to put his trousers on, when I know he can do it himself. I understand that this is probably because he sees me doing everything for his sister and it must be heartbreaking for him. He loses his temper, doesn't listen, tries to wind us up and sulks. We empathise, but feel that we are a bit judgemental and we are trying to change that. For example, we both sound cross instead of calm. I sometimes shout, but I do apologise. He is a wonderful little boy and I can feel as if we're ruining his childhood because he seems so unhappy. Then, in the midst of things, we get a glimmer of our happy, loving little boy. School says that he's great there and he doesn't seem as angry with other people.*

A: It sounds to me that your little boy is feeling very anxious about his place in your family and in your affections. This has also come at a time when other things are new in his world, particularly school and the change in sleeping arrangements. I think he is desperately trying to get more attention from you and he has quickly realised that the easiest way to do that is by doing things that you really dislike. Giving him as much attention as possible when he is calm is the way forward here. I can understand it is really difficult finding time for two children, particularly with one so young, but I think you need to work on being as attentive as possible before issues arise.

I would suggest that you make time each day that is just for your son. First, when your daughter sleeps, focus your attention on him. Next, when Dad is home ask him to go out for a walk with your daughter, leaving you at home with your son for a minimum of half an hour, but preferably longer. Alternatively, you can leave the house with your son while Dad stays home with your daughter. In this time, you concentrate on your son as much as possible and ask him what he would like to do. You could also give this daily 'Mum-and-son' time a name, such as 'our time', so that he can look forward to it when you refer to it during the day. It is very important that it is just the two of you at this time. Wearing your daughter in a sling when it happens doesn't count. This should make a large difference to his behaviour and will also help you to see how wonderful he is again.

In the meantime, when he hits his sister I would firmly say, 'Stop. I won't let you hit your sister', then pick him up and move to a sofa with him and sit down. Explain to him why he cannot hit her, that you can see he is angry and would he like your help to calm down? The natural instinct here may be to pick up your daughter and send your son away; however, this only reinforces the fact that you and she are a team, with him excluded. So try to soothe your daughter as quickly as possible, but focus on your son.

In terms of spitting, I would redirect and say: 'You can't spit on the floor, but you can do it in the sink. Shall I come with you to the bathroom?'

It's normal for a child to lose their temper at this age. Your son is only four. I can understand that that seems very big when you have a baby too, but it really isn't. His brain is still very immature and he will find it very, very difficult to control his emotions. You need to help him to understand that it's OK to be mad and sad, but that it's not OK to hit or spit. If he cries, comfort him and say, 'You're really angry. I can see that. It's OK to cry – sometimes it really helps.' It sounds to me as if he has a lot of tears he needs to shed. The more you allow him to cry, the less he will hold the feelings inside and be prone to erupting.

Q: *When my daughter, who is five and a half, gets angry, she lashes out, almost instinctively. She has hit both of us and also her brother, who is four years younger. That particularly saddens me, as I don't want this issue to damage their relationship. I also don't want him to think that violence is the way to deal with angry feelings. It is also quite scary. Once she threw a shoe at my face and another time she punched me in the mouth and split my lip. She has hit one or two other people, although mostly it's us. I'm worried that she'll end up getting into fights when she's older. I really struggle with this, as I want to help her deal with her feelings, rather than punish her, but also make it clear that it is wrong. My husband isn't overly keen on gentle parenting, but it's definitely the way to go for me. What can we do to help her deal with her anger without hurting other people?*

A: First of all, I want you to understand that you haven't done something wrong, or made your daughter behave in this way. Violent children can really dent the confidence of parents and cause a great deal of anxiety.

Anger in itself isn't a problem; it's just an emotion like any other, so please don't make your daughter feel that it's wrong to be angry. It's how we express it that matters. You need to really stress this point to your daughter. It's OK that she has big feelings, and it's OK that she expresses them. In many ways, violence is a bit of a reflex response that tends to happen when we feel scared or threatened in some way. This fear can absolutely be psychological in cause and in many instances your daughter probably won't know why she is feeling like she is, as triggers can sometimes be subconscious.

I think first of all you need to look for anything that is triggering your daughter's behaviour. Does she find it hard to cope in certain places or environments? Is she affected by tiredness or hunger? Is she harder to handle if you have had your attention taken up by something else for a while, or after you have been away? Is something triggering the behaviour in school? Is she struggling with lessons or with friendships there? Is she perhaps being bullied? Next, you should really work on your connection with her. It isn't your daughter you dislike but her behaviour – these two are very different. Can you go out for the whole day with her, just the two of you, picking something fun to do? Spend time really working on your bond with her and help her to know that she can always talk to you and tell you what she's feeling and ask you for help.

Next, you need to explain to her how her actions make other people feel. At this age she still doesn't have very good empathy skills, so she may not realise the full extent of her actions. Then it's time to have a talk with her about how she can manage her anger in more acceptable ways. Help her to notice how she feels when she starts to get angry. Does she feel her breathing speed up? Does she become tense? Does she get a dry mouth? Does she start to feel hot? If she is aware of the early-warning signs she has more of a chance of controlling her response. Now come up with some ways in which she can work to decrease her anger without lashing out. This is about helping her to come up with alternative responses, which may include:

- breathing in and out very slowly while she counts to ten

- closing her eyes and imagining something that makes her really happy

- pressing the thumb and forefinger of her right hand onto the soft section of skin between the thumb and forefinger on her left hand

- pinging a rubber band on her wrist

- squeezing some putty or Play-Doh in her pocket

- repeating the words 'I am calm, I am calm, I am calm', over and over again in her mind

- closing her eyes and picturing an 'anger dial' in her mind, imagining slowly turning down the dial, from the very red 'angry' part to the blue 'calm' part.

Or perhaps she may come up with her own ideas.

The next time you see her becoming angry, step in and remind her: 'It's OK to be angry. Remember our special technique we spoke about? Shall I help you to do it now?' Or, if you don't catch her in time, calmly move her away from the injured party or, if it's you, gently hold her hands and say, 'I won't let you hit – it hurts.' Then say, 'It's OK you are angry, but it's not OK to hurt people', then move on to reminding her about her technique and asking if she wants your help to calm down.

While it may be tempting to exclude her from the rest of the family or punish her in some way, especially if your husband isn't naturally 'gentle' in discipline style, ultimately, it won't teach her anything. Punishment creates more of a disconnect between you and may make her behaviour even worse. Working with anger gently is a long-term process, so don't expect things to change overnight. If you are consistent, however, you will see changes over the coming months. Remember though, you are not looking at extinguishing the anger and always keeping her calm. That's unrealistic. You are looking at teaching her how to control her anger in ways that don't harm others, or indeed herself.

Being the parent of 'a violent child' can be really tough. Far too many parents blame themselves and feel embarrassed about their child's behaviour. In reality, however, almost all children are violent at some point. They all struggle with emotion regulation and, as such, lashing out physically can be considered normal behaviour for this age. There are always triggers underlying the behaviour, and finding these is the key to resolving it. Once you know what your child's trigger is you can work on helping them to manage their emotions in a more socially acceptable way, if not extinguish the behaviour naturally. The results may not be as quick as you would like (in a way, you are working against biology), but don't lose hope. The techniques in this chapter will work if you stay calm, remembering SPACE, as discussed in the Introduction, and, most importantly, consistent, even if you feel like giving up.

Chapter 7

Coping with Whining and Sulking

Whining is an almost inevitable part of childhood. 'Mummeeeee ... Daddeeeee ... pleeeeease ... ' or, 'But why? I don't want to. I want you to do it' are almost guaranteed to be heard in your home at some point – more likely than not in a high-pitched, whiny voice that gets to you in the same way as nails being dragged down a blackboard.

On the opposite end of the scale is 'the sulk': a child with a face like thunder, arms crossed resolutely across their chest, immovable, with tightly zipped lips. When you try to speak to them they turn their head the other way, loudly blow out air through their noses or heavily flop down onto their bed or sofa in a dramatic fashion.

I was a master sulker when I was younger. I was never verbally rude or violent, but I would storm loudly up the stairs, fling open and then almost, but not quite, slam my door shut, before dramatically draping myself across my bed, face down. I would stay like this for hours on end. Each minute that I sulked, however, I would silently beg for my parents to come and see if

I was OK. My anger masked a desperate need to be understood, supported and loved, especially when I was a teenager. When you are a tween or a teen, your parents' attention and treatment of you is directly linked to their love for you – or at least that's what you think. Of course, in reality, it isn't, but in the mind of a teenager it almost always is. My sulks were always a cry for attention and connection. I certainly didn't enjoy them. Feeling desperately sad, angry and out of control isn't something that you do purely to 'wind up' or manipulate your parents. Sulking really doesn't feel good for the sulker.

I was never much of a whiner, but I would imagine the feelings are the same. At least when my own children whine, I can tell that they aren't feeling good, that there is an underlying dis-ease. And despite the nerve-jangling effects of their whining, I try my hardest to view it as a communication that all is not well in their lives. The indisputably best way to lessen and cope with sulking and whining is to understand the reasons behind them. Fix the feelings and you have little else to do.

Once again, when you are working out how to deal with a child who whines or sulks, ask yourself: Why? How? What?

- Why are they acting in the way that they are? Can you spot any triggers?

- How are they feeling? (The chances are, not particularly good.)

- What do you hope to teach them when you discipline them?

Why do children sulk and whine?

Children whine and sulk for many different reasons; however, there are some that are fairly universal. While whining and sulking may seem very different, both centre around a child perceiving a lack of control and a feeling of powerlessness – the overwhelming feeling of not being listened to or respected and a lack of connection with their parents. In almost all cases, the child is suffering in some form.

In this chapter we will look at the most common reasons for sulking and whining and how to reduce them using a mindful and gentle approach to discipline.

Lack of control

Perhaps the top reason why a child whines and sulks is because they struggle for control over their daily lives and environments, and these are often expressions of their feelings of powerlessness. When children of any age feel powerless to control situations, whining and sulking are prevalent. They know that there is nothing they can do to control the situation, and so regular communication is pointless. Whining and sulking are almost admissions from the child that they have 'lost', even before negotiations begin, and are not happy with the outcome. Here, remember the 'control' trigger we looked at in Chapter 1, which you can refer back to for a deeper understanding of the effects of a lack of control (see page 27).

Lack of communication skills

For younger children, particularly toddlers and preschoolers, language acquisition is often not on a level with the emotions that they experience. If a child cannot vocalise how they are feeling, particularly if they are feeling bad, the chances are they will whine, sulk or both. Can you imagine how frustrating it must be to feel sad, angry, anxious or tired and not be able to vocalise your needs to the people caring for you?

Lack of emotion regulation

We covered this in Chapter 1 and learned that toddlers, teenagers and children of every age in between struggle to regulate their behaviour. The frontal cortex of the brain – responsible for helping them to form rational conversations – is not yet fully developed, which results in whining or dramatic displays of feelings, such as tantrums. The immature brain development also means that once they are behaving in this manner, they are almost incapable of stopping.

Feeling overwhelmed

Children can feel overwhelmed for all sorts of reasons: at home they could feel overwhelmed by the requests you make of them; at school they can feel overwhelmed with the work they are expected to do, and the organisation required of them; in organised groups they can feel overwhelmed because of all the people around them; and in new environments they can feel overwhelmed by the sensory input. Feeling this way, particularly when they cannot control the situations they find themselves in, can leave children very prone to whining and sulking.

Being overtired

When a child of any age is overtired – whether from a lack of sleep from the previous night, because of focusing on exams, from running around lots or spending full days at nursery – behaviour almost always regresses. When this happens they tend to resort to whining in particular. As adults, we struggle to control our emotions when we are exhausted, so it's not surprising the same is true of children.

Not feeling heard

As with most undesirable behaviour, when a child feels a disconnect with their caregivers, whether they are parents, teachers or nursery workers, their behaviour regresses. So, if children don't feel listened to, they can quickly resort to whining or sulking. Conventional wisdom says to ignore them while they sulk or pay no attention to them when they whine. This is outdated advice, however, and is the worst thing you can do. Ignoring a child who is whining or sulking because they feel disconnected highlights the fact that you are not listening to them and increases their perceived lack of control over their life. Another common response to whining, namely 'I don't understand what you're saying, talk properly', makes children feel chastised and that their feelings are being ignored. Once again, this only increases the problem and is likely to result in even more whining and sulking in the future.

How do you stop whining and sulking?

Ultimately, time has the biggest impact. Both whining and sulking are behaviours that tend to be outgrown as the child approaches adulthood, although I'm sure everybody knows an adult who still whines or sulks!

In the meantime, there are several interventions that can ease the intensity and occurrences of whining and sulking – usually a combination is required. Here, we are still considering keeping a SPACE (see page 12) between your child's action and your reaction and keeping in mind the 'Why?', the 'How?' and the 'What?' in the scenario.

Listen intently

Connection almost always comes at the top of my list of recommendations for helping with undesirable behaviours. If your connection with your child is fractured for some reason, this should probably be your starting point. Take time to really listen to what your child is saying. Make eye contact when they speak, communicate with them at their level, physically and, whenever possible, make them the focus of your attention. When they speak to you repeat back what they are saying: 'OK, so you're feeling really grumpy that we have to stay home and tidy today, when you would like to go out.' Listening intently to what your child is saying or asking of you really helps to make them feel validated. Even if you cannot agree to their request, it can lessen the degree of whining and sulking hugely. Remember that even if what they are whining about may seem trivial to you, it is still really important in their world, so don't be tempted to belittle their wishes or concerns. As the author Catherine M. Wallace said:

> Listen earnestly to anything your children want to tell you, no matter what. If you don't listen eagerly to the little stuff when they are little, they won't tell you the big stuff when they are big, because to them all of it has always been big stuff.

They may be whining about the colour of their cup, while you are worrying about paying the rent or the mortgage, but it matters to them just as much as your concerns matter to you.

If your child has a habit of whining when they want your attention, but you are busy – especially when you are speaking to somebody in person or on the telephone – it is very important that you make them feel heard. Rather than ignoring them or saying, 'Wait a minute, I'm busy', excuse yourself from your conversation temporarily and say: 'I hear you. You are getting bored waiting; I will do my best to finish up quickly.' You may have to repeat this a couple of times, but just showing that you understand that your child is bored can really help to give them a little more patience to wait.

Alternative communication

For younger children who struggle with communicating their feelings verbally, using non-verbal methods can make a huge difference. For toddlers, learning some basic sign language can be a big breakthrough. Using emotion flashcards (laminated cards with pictures of different emotions and the words underneath) can prove insightful. The child can sort through the cards and show you how they are feeling, even when they are unable to communicate this to you verbally. Encouraging children to draw pictures of how they feel can be enlightening too. You can also make up a secret language between you, for your child to let you know when they are feeling overwhelmed. For instance, squeezing your hand could mean 'I'm scared', touching the top of your leg could mean 'I'm bored' and putting their head on your leg could mean 'I'm sad'. These silent forms of communication can be really helpful when you are out in public, especially if your child is expected to keep quiet.

More autonomy

Helping children to feel that they have more power over their lives is one of the best ways to reduce whining and sulking. More autonomy doesn't mean that you have to always let them do what they want – far from it. You do, however, need to allow them to have as much control as possible, adapting as they grow older. When trying to give them more control, it is important to understand that it is not given through forced choices. Asking 'This or this?' does not give the child control. I always liken it to going out for dinner and being given a menu that only has two dishes on it. You would think, Well, this is a poor restaurant – they have no choice at all. And that is the same fake 'choice' many parents offer their children.

Here are some ways you can give your child more autonomy. Boundaries can be put in place for all of these; you do not need to give them full control:

- Control over what, when and how much they eat

- Control over what they wear

- Control over their free time and activities

- Control over their friendships

- Control over family activities

- Control over their hairstyle

- Control over their personal hygiene

- Control over their bedroom décor

More downtime

When children are tired or overwhelmed, scheduling some downtime into their day can have a wonderful impact. Create a space in your house that can be used as a 'chill-out area' (under the stairs works really well). Put a couple of bean bags there, some squishy cushions, some fairy lights, blankets, books and a CD or MP3 player (relaxation or mindfulness CDs are very effective). When your child seems tired or overwhelmed, but not ready to sleep, suggest that they go to the chill-out area, either with or without you (their choice). Scheduling in fifteen minutes every day for downtime can have a really positive effect on whining and sulking.

More physical connection

Touch is a great regulator for children. A hug can help at any age, even if your older child initially shrugs you off. Roughhousing, play fighting and general 'goofing around' can help to draw you closer, as can play. For younger children, getting down on the floor with them, building bricks or train tracks, playing with dolls or painting and drawing are great ways to connect in close proximity with each other. For older children, a shared game on a console, going out to see their favourite band in concert or a trip to see the latest blockbuster at the cinema with dinner beforehand can be a good ice-breaker.

Encourage emotion release

Whining and sulking can often be caused by storing up emotions. Just like us, if children become too 'full up' with uncomfortable feelings, they may explode or become grumpy, irritable and whiny. If your child is particularly sulky or whiny and the previous tips don't help, it's likely that they need an emotional release. In this case 'needing a good cry' is very much applicable. Encouraging children to communicate their feelings and release them safely in your company can be really cathartic for you both.

Parents can unwittingly cause children to store up emotions. If your child does tend to retain difficult feelings, a quick analysis of your communication is probably in order. Instead of telling them, 'Come on, don't cry', or, 'Don't be silly, stop crying', or, 'You're a big boy/girl now', use phrases such as, 'It's OK, you can cry all you need', 'Sometimes it feels good to cry and let it all out', or, 'You're never too old to cry – I'm here for you.'

Real family case study

I would like to end this chapter on some real communication between myself and a mother who was concerned about her son's whining. Again, the question is about a child of a specific age, but my answer can be applied to any age. As you read through the question and my response, ask yourself about the 'Why?', the 'How?' and the 'What?'

> Q: *My son has just turned five and is a big sulker over small things. If he doesn't get the new spoon or the blue bowl at breakfast, he will start crying and sulking and stamping his feet until he can find one to wash or until I walk out of the room and he can eat his breakfast without me watching him using the other spoon. This is a daily occurrence and now our three-year-old is copying the behaviour.*

A: It sounds as if your little boy is feeling a bit powerless. I don't think the problem is the spoon or bowl per se – they are symptoms of how he is feeling. I would give him as many opportunities to be in control as possible. At breakfast, for instance, I would ask him to get the bowls and spoons out for both him and his sibling and get him to carry them to the table. I would have specific crockery and cutlery that is his and his only. Go on a shopping trip together and allow him to choose his own special bowl and spoon and make sure that nobody else in the house is allowed to use them. I suspect there are other ways you can help him to regain some control over his life too, such as creating a space in the house that is solely his – somewhere he can retreat to if he's feeling a little overwhelmed, angry or sad.

I also recommend that you allocate thirty minutes per day to play with him one on one, perhaps if your younger child still has a nap or, if you have a partner, when they are around. During this time, you should get down on his level and play games; roughhousing is also great here.

Lastly, when he is upset about something, such as not getting the right spoon, remember that at that specific moment in time, that spoon is as important to him as the most important thing in your own world. I know it can be really frustrating for you, but try to understand that he isn't behaving in that way to deliberately wind you up. In cases where you cannot give him control and need him to use the spoon (or any other object), you need to empathise with him: 'You really wanted the red spoon, didn't you? It sucks when you don't get to use the cutlery you want, doesn't it?' Then go on to set and reinforce your boundary: 'I can't let you have it this time, but tomorrow you can pick first.' At this point, you may want to offer an alternative to cheer him up a little: 'To cheer you up, how about we make cakes when we're all at home tonight?'

Helping your son to feel heard can go a long way to reducing his sulks. However, he is still very young and this sort of behaviour is really indicative of the immature brain development that is normal for his age. When you have a younger child, it can be easy to expect too much of your eldest, just because you see them as 'big'. But he simply isn't capable of the sort of emotion regulation needed to override this behaviour right now. Listening to him, supporting him and allowing him to have as much autonomy as possible will aid the development of emotion regulation as he grows.

Sometimes, I think we expect behaviour from children that we don't always display ourselves. I know many adults who whine and sulk if they aren't happy or don't get their way, myself included, actually. It's lovely that we hold our children in such high regard, but ironic that we expect them to accept things that perhaps we ourselves wouldn't. Whining and sulking always have an underpinning trigger: what is your child trying to tell you? Find the trigger and you have found the 'What?' in your discipline conundrum. For children to behave better, they have to feel better. This is particularly true of the behaviour addressed in this chapter.

Chapter 8

Coping with Not Listening and Refusal to do Things

Children not listening and refusing to do what you have asked are universal parenting problems. Many parents contact me and tell me that they have asked their child to do something until they were 'blue in the face'. They tell me they have tried asking nicely, they have tried punishment, they have tried rewards and nothing works. They describe tantrums when they tell their children it's time to leave the park, turn off their games console or come in from the garden. They tell me that they feel powerless and hopeless, demotivated and disconnected from their children. The irony is, in most cases their children feel exactly the same.

So why don't children listen? A good way to answer this is to ask what stops you from listening to somebody? Imagine your boss, your mother or your partner was asking you to do something in such a way that made you feel angry, upset or confused. What might they be asking of you and in what way? I would certainly be far less likely to listen to someone or do what they were asking of me if they:

- shouted at me

- spoke to me with a lack of respect

- patronised or criticised me

- expected me to do something that they didn't do themselves

- wanted me to do something difficult, but weren't prepared to offer me any help

- were asking me to immediately stop doing something I was enjoying, with no reason as to why I had to comply right now

- required me to do something that they knew I wasn't capable of doing

- demanded something of me that they would never ask of my peers or siblings

- gave me confusing and unclear instructions

- showed little regard for my feelings.

As adults, if others show us a lack of respect and understanding, it is reasonable for us to ignore their requests. We could even respond by saying something like, 'Well, if you asked me nicely I might consider what you're asking, but I'm feeling a little disrespected here at the moment'; or we might say, 'I'm really busy right now. I can't do this yet, but remind me tomorrow and I may be able to help.' Can you imagine how you would respond if your child replied to you in a similar manner? I'm guessing you wouldn't be very happy. Some parents might say,

'Who do you think you are, speaking to me like that?' So why is it OK for adults to query what is being asked, but not children?

Why children don't listen

The next time you find that your child is not listening or refusing to do what you've asked, consider how you would feel in their position. Would you feel inclined to respond to somebody talking to you in the same way? Let's look at some common mistakes parents make when asking their children to do something.

Poor communication

If your child doesn't listen to you, there is a chance that you are not communicating effectively. One of the biggest mistakes parents make is telling their child what they don't want them to do, rather than what they do want them to do: 'Stop running', 'Don't touch that', 'Stop hurting the dog', 'Don't eat that.' There are two problems with this approach, the first being that children are far more likely to hear the second half of the command – 'running', 'touch that', 'hurting the dog' and 'eat that' – than the 'Stop' or 'Don't'. Second, and perhaps most important, is that when you give your child a negative command, you don't tell them what you want them to do instead.

Knowing that children of almost all ages have poor logical reasoning skills, we should always tell them what we want them to do. To you, the logical outcome of not running is to walk instead. You have reasoned that the appropriate response should be to slow down and that walking is a slow way of moving. To a child with a less developed frontal cortex, this is not so obvious. If you don't want them to run, what should they do? Should they skip? Jump? Hop? Crawl? Fly? Stand still? And what about 'Don't touch that'? There are two problems for the child here: their lack of impulse control and, again, the absence of logical reasoning skills, which we looked at in some detail in Chapter 3 (see pages 56–60).

If you rephrase it, replacing the negative command with a positive instruction, the child is much more likely to hear and respond. Some common examples can be seen in the table below.

Ineffective Negative Command	Effective Positive Command
Stop running.	Walk, please.
Don't touch that.	Hands by your side, please.
Stop pulling the cat's tail.	Gentle hands with the cat, please.
Stop walking away from me.	Stay with me and hold my hand, please.
Stop hitting your sister.	Kind hands, please.
Stop making a mess with your dinner.	Food on the plate, please.
Stop shouting.	Quiet voice, please.
Stop moving.	Still and calm, please.
Don't draw on the walls.	Draw on the paper, please.
Stop throwing.	Hold the ball still in your hand, please.

Remember always that you are acting as a role model when you discipline your child, and asking them to do something is no exception. Keep your voice calm and quiet. If you shout or raise your voice, your communication is far less likely to be effective – just as you wouldn't listen if your boss or partner shouted at you. Lastly, remember your body language: if you have a small child, crouch down to their level and look them in the eye, making contact with them too if possible – a hand on the shoulder or holding their hand.

Confusing instructions

How is your memory? If I asked you to close this book, go to your kitchen and get a spoon, then go to a drawer in another room and find a pair of scissors, then go to your wardrobe and get a jacket and bring them all back to the room you started off in, would you struggle to remember everything? I know I often find myself forgetting why I've gone into a room when it was only to get one thing, so how much more difficult must it be for a child with a far less developed brain to follow a series of complicated instructions, or even attempt to do so.

Giving your child only one thing to focus on, with a clear explanation, is communication at their level and thus far more likely to be listened to. Keep your questions and instructions short and clear and, most importantly, only give one command at a time: 'Please get your shoes', then, when they return, 'Please put your shoes on.'

Not age-appropriate

Asking a two-year-old to sit still and be quiet while they wait is most likely to end badly. It is not age-appropriate. At two years old a child has minimal impulse control and an overwhelming desire to move and make noise. You are doomed to failure from the off if your requests expect too much. Next time you struggle to get your child to listen to you or do what you've asked, remind yourself of what you learned about child brain development in Chapter 3 and whether what you are asking is age-appropriate.

Lack of fun

Childhood is all about play. Play is how children learn, how they connect and bond and how they communicate. Even when they are older, play is infinitely more appealing to them than boring, everyday chores. The next time you ask your child to do something, particularly if they are engrossed in play of some form, consider how you can make what you are asking of your child more fun. Can you turn your request into a game? A race? A song? Can you make it funny? The table below gives you some ideas.

Request	Fun Solution
Putting toys away	Make a 'goal' and throw the (soft!) toys through the goal into the toy box. Keep a tally of how many goals are scored and see if they have beaten their top score from yesterday.
Putting coat on	Turn it into a race: who can put theirs on first? Who will be the grand 'Coat-putting-on-champion' your house will cheer for?
Tidying up dinner plates	Sing a silly tidying-up song together. 'This is the way we tidy the dinner, tidy the dinner, tidy the dinner. This is the way we tidy the dinner, because we're a tidy-up winner.'
Brushing teeth	Pretend to be a dinosaur dentist checking for hidden leaves and bones stuck in their teeth. Ask them to open wide and roar loudly while you check with the dinosaur bone-cleaner brush.
Finding their shoes	Imagine they are on an expedition, looking for a lesser-spotted shoe monster. Who is going to be the greatest explorer and find them?
Getting ready for bed	Speak in a funny voice as if you are a crazy nanny from a different country who will tickle them if they are not in bed quickly.

| Bringing toys in from the garden | Pretend that there is a huge storm coming and they will be stranded in the garden in a huge flood unless they are quick (with an occasional spray of the hosepipe). Can they get inside before the flood comes? |
| Doing homework | Pretend that they are the teacher and you are the student and they are teaching you and planning today's lesson. They have to answer the questions to know the answer before they test you and take your answers in to mark. |

Lack of control

One of the top reasons why children refuse to listen and respond to requests from their parents is because they feel powerless. Again, the problem of lack of control we discussed in Chapter 1 rears its head. This is especially true if they are engrossed in a game, book or film on the television. In many ways, they are at your mercy when it comes to how they spend their free time. When they ask you to do something, do you ever ask them to wait until you have finished what you're doing? Yet when the situation is reversed might you ask them to do something 'now'. Can you imagine how frustrating it must be to have so little control? Would you feel inclined to ignore a request too in that situation? If, however, you say, 'I want you to tidy your room today; when would you like to do it?' you give them some much needed autonomy which will, in turn, increase the likelihood of them listening and responding.

Lack of connection

Your communication should not just convey your intentions, but also your connection with your child. The more connected they feel to you, the more likely they are to listen. In Chapter

1, we discussed a feeling of disconnect as a trigger for undesirable behaviour – an idea that we need to pick up on again here. Whenever you are unhappy with your child's behaviour, remind yourself that it is only their behaviour that you do not like. That is separate from your love and affection for them. Very often parents find themselves shouting, shaming and threatening if their children ignore them or refuse to do what they ask. These techniques may work, but if they do, they will generate a very superficial and short-term reaction that will actually make it less likely that the child will listen in the future. Having a good connection with your child will make them more inclined to do what you ask for no reason other than that they love you.

Lack of empathy and understanding

How would you feel if you were engrossed in a book or conversation, or in the middle of doing something you felt was important, and your partner demanded your instant attention and co-operation? Very often, we speak to children and ask them to do things in a way that we ourselves would dislike. In Chapter 3 we looked at the importance of empathy, and the same applies again here. If your child is engrossed in an activity, it is far better to say, 'I can see that you're very busy at the moment, and I don't want to interrupt your fun, but I do need to ask you to put your shoes away. Would you prefer to do it now, so you can get straight back to what you're doing? Or finish up in the next five minutes so that you can do it then?' This is preferable to: 'I've told you to do it now. Why don't you ever listen? I said *now*.' Both requests are essentially the same, and make the same demand of the child, but the way they are phrased shows a huge difference in understanding and empathy on the part of the parent.

Common 'refusing-to-do-something' struggles

Next, let's look at some common scenarios that parents often struggle with and suggested ways to handle them. As you read these scenarios, remember to think about the 'Why?', the 'How?' and the 'What?' in each case:

- Why is the child behaving in this way?

- How are they feeling?

- What are you hoping to teach them with your discipline?

Refusal to go to sleep

Bedtime struggles are commonly perceived to belong firmly in the baby and toddler years. What most parents of young children don't realise, however, is that they can continue for many years. The teenage years, in particular, can often bring about many bedtime issues, with children often refusing to go to bed at a time that the parent deems suitable.

Let's start with the 'Why?' here. One of the biggest problems when it comes to sleep is that children are not always biologically ready to go to bed when their parents expect them to. As we've already seen, from the age of two to nine or ten years of age a realistic bedtime is around 8 or 9 p.m. Before this it is quite likely that their bodies have not secreted sufficient melatonin (the hormone of sleep), and sleep will be tricky for them. Younger children can also really struggle with reconnecting with their parents after day care or school and are often resistant to going to bed until they have spent enough time at home in the evening reconnecting after a day away. For those parents who work, children need to spend at least two hours doing this before the bedtime routine starts.

Teens often need significantly later bedtimes than their parents believe appropriate. From age eleven onwards bedtime starts to slowly creep backwards. For ten-, eleven- and twelve-year-olds a bedtime of around nine o'clock is appropriate and from thirteen onwards ten o'clock is most in sync with what is happening with their circadian rhythm or body clock. This does, of course, mean that many are tired in the morning and would prefer to sleep in later. They are not being lazy, however; this is simply a result of biology.

Now, let's think about how the child is feeling. As a parent, you probably relish an early night to relax and catch up on sleep. As a child, however, being sent to bed before they are tired is not a recipe for success. In fact, going to bed when they're not tired can often mean ending up stressed and full of cortisol as a result. Cortisol inhibits melatonin, which is why insomniacs are recommended to stop *trying* to get to sleep. Bedtime also usually involves the child being in a room alone, away from their parents. For many this is a scary concept and they will try as hard as they can to stay with their parents for as long as possible, resisting bedtime. In most cases, bedtime refusal isn't an act of defiance, but a way of asking for more time with you and not to be alone.

Next, let's think about what you hope to achieve when it comes to sleep and discipline. Of course your primary goal is probably that your child gets the amount of sleep that they need, to keep them healthy and happy. Sometimes, parents want their children to go to bed so that they can have more of an evening to themselves, which is not a great reason. Teaching your child good sleep hygiene and helping them to relax and have good sleep associations is really important. Most parents don't speak to their children about sleep and the effects on their body, but this really should be the starting point: explaining how sleep heals the body and the mind and helps them to have energy for the next day, as well as an explanation of what happens when they don't get enough sleep. Next comes making the sleep environment a place where they feel comfortable and calm; and working on an excellent bedtime routine, especially if they are younger. A routine helps the child to know that bedtime is approaching and to feel in control, knowing what to expect and when.

Lastly, boundaries are important, especially when they are enforced consistently. Letting your child stay up one night and not the next does not work. Setting a bedtime that is adhered to as much as possible is key. If your child is reluctant to go to bed, always start by empathising with them ('I understand you don't want to go to bed right now . . . ') and then explain why it is necessary ('but do you remember when we talked about how important sleep is?'). Lastly, allow them to have some control over the process: 'Would you like to read for ten minutes in bed? Or would you like me to put some music on for you to listen to as you go to sleep?'

So keeping to a regular bedtime, helping the child to understand the importance of sleep and a biologically appropriate bedtime, and implementing a good, solid, predictable routine are crucial in solving problems around going to sleep.

Refusal to tidy their room

Let's face it, most people really don't like tidying up. I certainly don't, and I can totally understand that most children dislike it too. Room tidying does have to happen though, so how do you make it less painful?

Again, let's start with the 'Why?' Why do children refuse to tidy their rooms? First, obviously, is that it is really not an enjoyable task. So making it more fun is a great solution. Crank up some music to dance to, make it into a race with other siblings tidying their rooms or join your child and view it as a great bonding time – as well as the fact that two pairs of hands speed up the work.

Tidying also often takes children away from what they would rather be doing. Scheduling in 'tidy-up time' once a week, so that it becomes part of their routine is a good way to get around this. The more it becomes part of everyday life, the easier children will find it. Also, from a practical point of view, try to make things easier for your children to tidy. Get lots of storage boxes and find homes for as much as possible, taking into consideration their ability to reach things and put them away. My own children found it quite difficult to put clothes on hangers and put them in their wardrobes, so we ditched the wardrobes and got large chests of drawers instead, which has definitely taken some of the stress out of putting clothes away.

It's also a good idea to tell your children *why* they need to tidy. Showing them photographs of dust mites can be quite effective, explaining that if the floor is not clear it can't be hoovered and it will quickly become dirty and full of tiny little critters. You can also point out that it is much easier for them to find their belongings and have space to entertain, draw, play and do their homework if it is tidy.

Next, think about how they are feeling. Most people don't like tidying, so empathise with them: 'I really don't like cleaning either; it's boring isn't it?' You could also suggest something fun you can do when they have finished: 'Shall we get this done as quickly as possible and then go out to lunch together?' Allowing your child to have more control also helps: 'Your room needs tidying; you could do it tonight and have the day clear tomorrow, or do what you'd like to do tonight and then do it tomorrow. Which would you rather do?' This often works much better than you deciding when they should tidy.

It is important that you don't reward your child for tidying their room. Every time you bribe them with gifts and money you erode their intrinsic motivation (see page 75) and they will become less likely to tidy of their own accord. Tidying is part of living as a family. Everybody should be responsible for helping; you are not rewarded as an adult and they shouldn't be either.

Lastly, think about what you want to achieve when you discipline for room tidying. Do you want to teach your child to just tidy their room while they live with you? Or would you like them to understand the virtues of cleanliness and tidiness for the years to come, even when they no longer live with you? Your approach will likely be quite different depending on what you aim for. If you would like them to become an adult who is mindful of their surroundings, then you have to help them to understand why it is important that they tidy and what happens if they don't? What do you want your child to learn from you? If you want them to tidy their room, then your own room has to be tidy too.

Refusal to put shoes on

Do you struggle to get your toddler to put their shoes on? Or perhaps you have a child who is always losing their shoes, resulting in a panicked hunt and late arrival at school?

Why is this? For toddlers it may be because they don't like the feel of shoes on their feet. Allowing them to go barefoot as much as possible, or buying special barefoot shoes can help to fulfil their sensory needs. There may also, again, be a control issue. Switching from laces to Velcro straps can give them more autonomy, reducing the need for your intervention and the time taken to put the shoes on. Lastly, think about your communication: are you giving your child too many commands at once? ('Go to the cupboard, get your shoes, bring them here and sit down so I can put them on you.') As discussed earlier, stick to one instruction at a time.

In terms of the child's feelings, they are likely to include stress from being rushed and a feeling of powerlessness for not being able to put on – or even find – their shoes. Reducing the stress and increasing autonomy are therefore crucial.

For older children who always lose their shoes or sit on the sofa shoeless as you are about to leave for school, this is largely about helping them to understand why their lack of shoes is a problem. Explain what happens when they are late and how stressed it makes you feel and, as a result, how it upsets them. Next, help them to take more control. Think about keeping a shoe box or shelf right next to your front door where they can put their shoes as soon as they come home, so that they know where they are the next day. Then make sure you allow plenty of time in the morning, so that there is no rush, and encourage them to have a routine to follow. You could even make up a rhyme: 'Breakfast first, it's time to eat. Then shoe time next, on your feet.'

Lastly, what do you want your child to learn from your discipline? To be organised so that they can get out of the door in time for school? Or that they need shoes on to protect their feet? Natural consequences could work quite well for the latter. If your toddler is refusing to put their shoes on, you could allow them to walk barefoot for a little while, until they realise the stones hurt their feet or the cold makes them sting. Of course, this would depend on the environment you are in and any risks presented (and you should also take the shoes with you for when they realise their mistake). For older children, perhaps tweens and teens, you could let logical consequences come into play. If they do not put their shoes in the box or on the rack and they cannot find them in the morning, they will have to wear non-uniform shoes and they may get told off at school. Again, adopt this approach carefully as it can backfire and create even more of a problem.

Refusal to do homework

Homework can be the bane of many a family. I am firmly of the opinion that most of it is completely pointless and doesn't add to a child's education at all, particularly during the earlier school years. For homework that does need to be completed, however, you often need a game plan.

Why don't children like doing homework? I'm not sure that this question really needs answering! After a busy day at school what most children want to do is relax at home and play with their friends. For older children in particular there are often three main things lacking when it comes to homework: organisational skills, understanding and control. Let's go through these in turn.

Most school-age children aren't particularly organised due to an immature frontal cortex. This is a simple case of brain development, and finding a system to help them work around it is one of the best things you can do. If your child doesn't already have a homework diary, try getting them one, so that they can note down their assignment and the date it is due. Some in- and out-trays can also be useful – the in-tray being for homework that needs to be done and the out-tray for work that is complete. Encourage your child to put the books in the trays in order of when the homework needs to be done, soonest on the top of the pile. A good workspace is important too: a desk with an organiser (containing pens, pencils, erasers, rulers, a stapler and paper clips) and a good light source. And you should help your child to set a routine to follow every afternoon, including sorting their homework and packing their bag back up the night before, so that there is no panic in the morning.

Refusal to do homework can also be an early sign that a child is struggling in a particular subject and they don't want to do their assignment simply because they don't understand it. If this is the case, urge them to seek help from the teacher or write a note in their book putting the teacher in the picture. Too many parents complete their children's homework in a bid to 'get it done', but this doesn't help anybody, least of all the child. If there is a problem, then it is important that their teacher knows.

Lastly, children can really feel powerless when it comes to schoolwork and the fact that once they are home their time still isn't their own. Setting a designated homework hour can be really helpful, so that they know they are free before five and after six, for example, but can really focus on their homework during that hour. Otherwise, if children procrastinate over homework it can feel like it lasts for ever.

Next, think about how your child feels. Often they can feel sad and frustrated when it comes to homework. Empathising is once again key: 'You're feeling really annoyed you have to do your homework now. I would probably feel the same.' However, explaining to them why they have to work hard now is also important. Talking about what they would like to do when they are an adult, and what they have to achieve to get there (plus, what happens if they don't) can often be a good driver to motivate children. (This can apply to any child from age five and above.) If they are struggling in a subject, talk to them about growth mindsets (see page 42) and how their abilities aren't fixed, but are a result of their thinking and effort. Talk about your own years at school and what you struggled with, and, most importantly, what you achieved. And make sure that your child has lots of free time to unwind, with no homework and no organised activities.

Lastly, think about what you hope to get from your discipline. Do you want your child to be an effective learner in their own right? If so, your aim is to help them to take control of their learning and increase their organisational skills, not focusing on any one specific piece of homework. Try to rein yourself in when it comes to completing homework for them; think of the bigger picture and how, in the grand scheme of things, it doesn't really help them. Sometimes, we have to let children make their own mistakes in order for them to learn.

Refusal to turn off the games console

Consoles and other screen time can be one of the most difficult parts of family life. The games themselves are designed to be highly addictive, and even as adults we can find managing our own time on them challenging.

Aside from the addictive nature of the games, one of the reasons why children right through to young adults in their early twenties find limiting screen time so difficult is their lack of impulse control (see page 57). Knowing how difficult it is as an adult to shut down a game and not spend 'just five more minutes' trying to win, think how much harder it is for your child. Imagine you were just about to win a race or defeat a baddy and your partner yells out, 'Come on, turn it off now.' Would you reply, 'Just a minute, I can't now'? Then what if they said, 'I told you to turn it off *now*'? And what if you were so nearly there, doing so much better than you had ever done before in the game and your partner stormed in, turned the console off and sent you to your room, banning you from playing on it for the next week? You never made a conscious decision to be 'naughty', nor did you mean to be rude or disrespectful; it's just that the game filled you with adrenaline, a fight-or-flight response you might say, and you yelled or slammed the door on your way out because of the physical and chemical changes within your body. This is what millions of children around the world experience every day and, as parents, you have to understand that this response is not personal.

But what should you do? Putting firm screen/game time boundaries in place is important. As I mentioned earlier, in my house we have a maximum of one hour's screen time per day on weekdays (I know that my children can't handle the effects when they have to get up early the next day), and at weekends they are limited to two hours each per day. It is not a popular boundary, but one that they have grudgingly accepted after I have spent many hours explaining the negative effects of screen time to them. I have shared articles about what it does to their brains, pointed out the behaviour of others and helped them to notice the same in themselves. This is so important – unless you explain the effects and the reasons behind your actions your children will just view you as a killjoy. Once they appreciate that you are regulating their behaviour for their own benefit, acceptance is more likely to follow. In the early days I used to keep the controllers in a secret place because I know how tempting it is to sneak on to a game. I now empathise through their anger and their tears, but I stay consistent. If they overstep a boundary and stay on too long, I make them aware that their time is up, then a logical consequence follows. I try to allow my children some input into their own consequences which, in the case of screen time, is always a restriction of their allocation whenever they next play.

I'm not a huge fan of consequences as a first-line approach when it comes to discipline, particularly for younger children. However, when it comes to screen time I feel they are almost essential.

Real family case studies

Once again, I would like to end the chapter with some correspondence from parents about situations they are finding difficult with their own children. The questions relate to children of a specific age, but my answers apply to any age group. As you read through them, see if you can identify the cause of the behaviour (the 'Why?'), an understanding of how the child feels (the 'How?') and what a good discipline solution would be (the 'What?').

Q: *I really need help getting my reluctant toddler to brush his teeth. It is always a struggle, as he totally refuses to let me do it. Every time we try it ends in tears.*

A: There are several reasons why toddlers don't like having their teeth brushed, but there are three main ones in my opinion. First, it makes them feel completely out of control (how would you feel if somebody tried to put a toothbrush in your mouth and brushed your teeth, especially if you didn't want it done?). Second, it disrupts what they are doing, which is most likely something that is much more fun. And lastly, there is something about the sensation of it that they dislike.

The answer to most tooth-brushing woes is to come up with a solution that considers all three causes. I always suggest that reluctant toddlers brush their own teeth, even if that only involves chewing on a toothbrush for a minute. The alternative here is to allow them to brush your teeth while you brush theirs. Taking turns to brush for just a few seconds or so can allow them to feel that they have some power over the situation. Next, don't aim for a specific tooth-brushing time and think about doing it in a different place: brushing while in the bath often works well, as does tooth brushing while watching a favourite video clip or reading a book. Lastly, investigate different types of toothbrushes – chewable rubber ones are often more successful and some toddlers love electric ones. Dental wipes are good too. You might also want to try a fruit-flavoured toothpaste or other alternative instead of mint.

Q: *How do I encourage my four-year-old to work with me to tidy her toys away, when she responds to everything by blowing raspberries and saying, 'I don't want to'?*

A: There are two important points to understand here. First, tidying is really boring and almost everybody hates doing it. Second, everybody living in the house has a responsibility to keep it tidy.

Starting with point one, there are a few things to think about. How do *you* feel about tidying? Do you complain about having to do it? Do you make it sound like a horrible, tedious job? Or perhaps you're not so good at tidying yourself (I know I'm not). We have to understand how much our children look to us to work out how they should behave. If your house is messy, chances are that they will be messy. If you don't tidy away after yourself, you can't expect that your child will just because you've asked them – as the saying goes, 'Do as I do, not as I say.' If you make tidying seem like an arduous task, then your child will grow to hate it too. Try making up a 'tidy-up song' (the sillier the better). Or create a funny tidying dance. Make it into a race – which of you can put the most toys in a basket first? Or time her and see if she can beat yesterday's record.

Moving on to point two, it's important that your child understands that she is a part of your family and, as such, her responsibilities are very similar to those of anyone else in the house. The family as a whole needs to keep the house tidy – it's non-negotiable. This doesn't mean you can't empathise though: 'Oh, honey I know you don't want to tidy, but it does have to be done. How could I make it more fun for you?' Or: 'Sweetheart, I can see you really don't want to tidy now, but we can't get any more toys out unless these are put away. Would you like to pack up the cars or the crayons first?' On a related note, as tidying is something all family members should do it is important that you never bribe your child to do it. That means no rewarding with sweets, toys or pocket money. If you 'pay' her to tidy she will expect more and more rewards for everyday tasks and become far less likely to do them without payment. You really don't want to go there at such a young age. Lastly, it is important that you always stick to your rule of tidying toys consistently. If you're tired or busy one day, you must still ask your daughter to tidy. Don't be tempted to think you'll just leave it for today. This is confusing for her. If she gets away with it today, she will try to do so tomorrow, or you will be met with more resistance when you try to enforce the boundary having previously let it slip.

So to sum up: empathise, keep strict boundaries in place every single day, model the behaviour you want to see and make the process as co-operative and fun as possible.

Can you remember the last time you were asked to do something and you didn't do it? For me it happened only last night. I was tired and wanted to go to bed, so I didn't help my husband to fix our broken printer. He wasn't happy that he was left with no help, but he empathised with me and knew that I was tired after a busy day. We agreed that we would reschedule and fix the printer together at the weekend. This is how adults resolve problems of 'not listening'. It is rare that parents fix issues in the same way with their children, but there's no reason why it should be any different. Understanding and empathising with our children is absolutely vital. Once again, we tend to expect behaviour from them that we don't always show as adults. The 'Why?' and 'How?' are crucial. If you consider your child's feelings, respect them and communicate with them clearly and effectively, the problem of not listening will diminish drastically.

Chapter 9

Coping with Rudeness and Backchat

When were you last rude to somebody? Think back to that occasion and how you were feeling at the time. What caused the uncomfortable feelings in you that made you respond in a rude way towards them? Was it something they said, or something that they perhaps did or didn't do? Close your eyes and try to remember the sort of response that was triggered before you reacted. Perhaps your body felt tense? Perhaps you felt your teeth and jaw clenching? Perhaps you were holding your breath or felt yourself get hot? Perhaps your heartbeat quickened? Perhaps you were feeling a sense of disbelief, felt wronged, attacked or misunderstood?

I can tell you the last time it happened to me. I was picking my daughter up from school. I was in the car, having just been to the supermarket. The school is in a residential road of old houses with permit parking and just a handful of free bays that are always taken up by people who are shopping in the nearby town. There is a public car park close by, but because it offers free, unlimited daily parking by 8 a.m. it is always full of commuters working in the town. The only other place to park is a pay-and-display car park half a mile away from the school or the permit-holder-only spaces. I chose the latter that day, as do almost all of the other parents on the school run. We shouldn't park there, but we take our chances for five minutes. As I sat in the car waiting for my daughter to come out I saw a traffic warden walking up and down the street. She was new. Whereas her predecessor had avoided the road at school drop-off and pick-up, probably because of the wrath of all the angry parents temporarily parking there, this new traffic warden was clearly on a mission. As she walked up to my car, I felt myself tense. She asked me if I had a parking permit, which I clearly didn't, then told me to 'move on'. I asked her if she had any thoughts as to where I could wait for my daughter, and she suggested the car park. I told her that it was full of commuters and there were never any spaces, and she said I should park in the car park half a mile away. I asked if she had any children and if she would really do that herself. She curtly replied, 'I don't think that's any of your business.' I explained that I knew it wasn't her fault, but school pick-ups were almost impossible if you had to drive and that the previous traffic warden had avoided the road at school-run times. I knew I was in the wrong and in a space I shouldn't be in, but there was no warmth from her, no sign of humanity, no interest in my situation. She simply said, 'If you don't move, I will give you a ticket.' As I began to pull away, I saw her walk towards the cars of other parents on the school run and called out, 'I suspect you will have a similar reaction from the other parents, particularly if you take the same attitude with them.' Like I said, I knew I was in the wrong and that she was only doing her job, but there was a combination of four things at play: her attitude and total lack of empathy or understanding towards my situation, the stress that I was feeling at now being late to collect my daughter, a fair dose of cognitive dissonance (more of which on page 171) on my behalf and the feeling of being powerless to do anything. There was nowhere I could park and I couldn't stop her from giving me a ticket if I left the car where it was. These feelings are almost guaranteed to trigger less than sociable responses in us, regardless of age.

Why children are rude and talk back

As you may expect, there are several underlying reasons why these things happen. Let's look at them in a little more detail.

Lack of empathy and understanding

If somebody asks, or rather, tells you to do something with little regard for your feelings, your response is likely to automatically be negative. Imagine if your colleague ignores the fact you are in mid-conversation with somebody, for example, and says, 'Can you pick up the post and take it to the post box, please?' the chances are that you will respond with something like, 'I was speaking actually. Can you do it?' Or, if they were quite curt with their request, you might say, 'Why can't you do it? And next time please don't interrupt me.' The same is true of many of the requests we make of our children.

If your child perceives that you have a lack of understanding of their issues or a lack of empathy for how your request has made them feel, they may snap back at you. The more they perceive your communication to take no account of their feelings or position, the more their response is likely to be rude. All too quickly, exchanges can turn accusatory and frosty and, as a parent, it can be extremely hard not to take backchat personally and slide into a grumpy or angry mood yourself. When you do become exasperated and angry and yell at your child, you can expect even more rudeness and backchat. After all, wouldn't you behave that way yourself if you were in a similar position?

Taking your child's feelings into account can go a very long way towards solving the problem. Speak to them in a way you would like to be spoken to and try to avoid chastising and shaming them. If you are having a particularly tough time with them, explain how you feel: 'I have a really bad headache today and feel very grumpy. I don't want to lose my temper with you, so please would you take your bag up to your room quickly?' Empathising with their feelings can be very powerful too: 'I know you wanted to go out with your friends today; it must have made you very angry when I said no. I would certainly be grumpy in your position.' Now, going back to my scenario above, if the traffic warden had just said to me, 'I understand – it must be really difficult for you with no parking', I wouldn't have lost my temper with her.

Stress response

Many children are rude almost subconsciously as they respond from a heightened level of stress. I'm sure that you have experienced the feeling of being 'tightly wound' and ready to snap. Perhaps you weren't feeling too well, were worrying about paying some bills, had just heard some bad news about a friend or just had a day where everything was difficult and not going to plan. Just one last wind on that coil is enough to make you spring open and lose your temper with somebody. The same is true for children. They may not have the 'big' adult worries that we have, but that doesn't mean that they don't have big feelings, anxiety and stress. Friendship worries, school tests, concerns about something they have seen or heard on the news and situations at home can all cause children to feel short-tempered and highly strung. Asking them to do (or, indeed, not do) something can be the very last straw for them. So while you might think that asking them to turn the light off in the kitchen shouldn't cause such an extreme response – and you would be right – it was probably less than 10 per cent of what they have been holding inside, and just happened to be the thing that triggered the release of all their pent-up emotion.

The answer here is to encourage your child to talk to you about what they are feeling. Avoid saying things like, 'Oh, don't be silly, you'll be fine', or, 'You'll make up tomorrow, don't worry about it; you'll be friends again.' These sorts of comments dismiss your child's feelings and make them less likely to share them with you in the future. If they have been especially snappy or rude, pick your moment and try to encourage them to open up to you. A cuddle and a little talk at bedtime when they are feeling more relaxed can often prove quite enlightening and helpful for both of you, no matter how old they are. Rudeness and backchat may not be pleasant, but they are both indications that all is not right in your child's world and in your connection with them. Knowing this, the worst thing you can do as a parent is to snap back. It will only ever exacerbate things, as it fractures the connection and stresses them even more. As the adult, you have to diffuse the situation. Stay cool and model calmness to your child.

Powerlessness

Backchat in particular is a sure-fire sign that your child is feeling completely powerless. In many ways it is their attempt to try to control a situation that they have absolutely no power over and, more importantly, they know it. Childhood is inherently a time of little influence and many struggle with this. Although there may be situations when you, as the parent, have to take almost full control, you can still help your child to feel heard by listening to their point of view. For instance, if they ask to go somewhere that you do not feel is appropriate, tell them why you have made the decision and then ask them to explain how they feel about it. Encourage them to verbalise their disappointment and anger and tell them, 'It's OK that you're angry. I get angry when people tell me I can't do things.' Next, ask if there is something else they would like to do, or invite them to come up with some alternatives that might work for both of you. The more you can involve your child in decisions, the more in control they will feel and the less need there will be for them to talk back to you.

Cognitive dissonance

Cognitive dissonance occurs when we try to reduce the psychological dis-ease we feel on seeing or hearing something that makes us question our beliefs and actions. Often, this results in attacking the messenger and not the message, especially when the message itself seems sound. From a child's perspective, they can find themselves in this state quite frequently. Agreeing with you almost means admitting that they themselves were wrong and that's something that they – like many of us – find difficult. This is the exact position I found myself in with the traffic warden I mentioned at the start of this chapter. I knew I was wrong, but I tried to turn things around and made it about her. Yes, she lacked understanding and empathy, but she was inherently right. And I chose to focus on her lack of communication skills, rather than acknowledge that I was wrong.

Admitting that we are wrong is hard, no matter how old we are – particularly if it means reassessing our actions and our beliefs. To a degree, it takes a large amount of confidence and self-esteem – often lacking in children. It also means that you must feel in some way connected to the person involved, and certainly demands a degree of trust in them. As adults, we would not like to admit our mistake to a partner or friend if they retorted, 'I told you so'; it's no surprise, therefore, that children feel the same and try to cover up their cognitive discomfort with rudeness and backchat. For this reason, it is important to support your child and enable them to tell the truth, whatever that truth may be, knowing there will be no repercussions or lecturing from you. It is also a good idea to talk with them about how it's OK to be wrong – everybody is sometimes, including you. Helping your child to see that you are not perfect can make them more likely to open up to you.

Crossing the Rubicon

Have you heard anyone refer to 'the point of no return' – an imaginary point which, once passed, can never be returned to. When I was planning a family trip to Walt Disney World, Florida, I considered booking us on to a tour that shows the behind-the-scenes running of the place. Beneath the theme park, cleaners and maintenance staff, as well as multiple cast members playing the same characters, use the tunnels to navigate the park, giving an illusion of perfection and the impression that there is only one Mickey, one Cinderella, etc., even though they may appear in three different locations simultaneously. When you are five years old, you want to believe that there is only one Mickey Mouse, so in the end I decided against the tour, although, as an adult, I would have loved to have seen the internal workings of the busy park.

For children, this loss of magic and fantasy can be an everyday occurrence – only it manifests as the realisation that their parents aren't perfect; that they make mistakes and can sometimes let them down. It is often called 'crossing the Rubicon' – an allusion to the story of Julius Caesar and his army in the north-east of Italy crossing the shallow Rubicon river. This was considered an act of treason at the time, but ignoring this, Julius Caesar said, *'alea iacta est'* (meaning 'the die is cast') and went ahead, so moving past the point of no return. For children, this stage in their life often comes as they enter their tweens and teens. There is no more Santa Claus, no more Easter Bunny, no more Tooth Fairy and, instead, there is the recognition that the world is a scary and often horrible place. This point of no return for children is a bridge across the lands of childhood and adulthood. They no longer fully belong in one, but they have not yet reached the other. It is a state of limbo – one where they are not on an equal footing with you as an adult, but where their thinking is changing from that of a child. The ensuing frustration often gives way to rudeness and backchat as they attempt to assert the authority that they know they do not have.

How do you deal with rudeness and backchat?

As a parent, rudeness and backchat can be incredibly hard to handle, particularly if they happen in public. But, rather than seeing it as a case of your child deliberately trying to embarrass or anger you, aim to understand the underlying emotions. Working with these emotions is the key to reducing the severity and occurrence of the unreasonable behaviour.

Age-appropriate expectations

Is your child navigating their own Rubicon – struggling on the bridge between childhood and adulthood? Rudeness and backchat are characteristic of this journey. In many cases their behaviour may not be a reflection of you, but of the state of flux they find themselves in, and often it will dissipate with age and maturity.

Empathy

What is your child feeling? Are they feeling an uncomfortable level of dissonance? Do they know that they are wrong, but don't want to admit it because that also means admitting that you are right? Are they using rudeness and backchat as a protection mechanism for some big, uncomfortable feelings that they don't want to experience? Showing your child that you are big enough to handle their feelings and ready to listen can have a significant impact on their actions. Saying, 'I understand you're feeling really unhappy right now, do you want to have a chat?' to a child who has slammed the door and screamed, 'I hate you', is much more constructive than shouting after them about how rude they are.

Reduce stress

Rudeness and backchat can often be at their worst at times of stress – for example, if your child has had an argument with somebody at school, is sitting exams or something is happening within your family dynamics. Try helping them to manage their stress levels and unwind in a safe way. Taking time out together to snuggle on the sofa and watch a movie, going for a walk in a park or forest, roughhousing or listening to a relaxation CD together can all help to lower your child's adrenaline levels and switch them out of the fight-or-flight response that they may find themselves stuck in.

Admit your mistakes and stay calm

Adults are often not good at admitting their mistakes, especially to their children, but this is so important. If you have done or said something wrong, tell your child that you're sorry, tell them what you did wrong and what you will do to make it right. After all, this is ultimately what you want them to do, so how will they learn without a good role model? Now is your time to be the adult. Stay calm and control your temper – you need to model good communication skills to your child, both talking and listening. If you shout or get angry, your child is less likely to talk to you calmly and there is more chance that they will snap back at you.

Increase autonomy

As we've already seen, if children feel powerless, they are more prone to undesirable behaviour, and the more control they are allowed over their own lives, the less they will need to battle for it. Ask your child for their opinions and what they think could be done to keep you both happy. Come up with some house rules together and ask them to contribute to setting certain boundaries in the house. You could even have a special 'worry box' where they can post any worries and thoughts that they might feel uncomfortable talking to you about face to face, and promise that you will check the box once or twice per week. If you have an older child and their behaviour calls for a logical consequence, ask them for ideas as to what that should be, so that their discipline is, to an extent, self-led.

Real family case studies

To end this chapter, I have included some correspondence about rudeness and backchat from two families, along with my advice to them, which can be applied to any age. As you read it, see if you can identify the cause of the behaviour (the 'Why?'), an understanding of how the child feels (the 'How?') and what a good discipline solution would be (the 'What?').

> **Q:** *I have a very verbally advanced three-year-old who, up until recently, listened attentively and usually answered when being spoken to. Now he doesn't seem to listen to anything, needs to be asked five or six times to do something and often I have to get him to stop what he's doing and ask him again. Also, if he doesn't like or want to do something, his default response seems to be shouting. This feels like a personal attack and I don't know how to help him and keep my cool at the same time.*

> **A:** I think the first thing to remember is that your son is only three years old. In brain-development terms he's really tiny, with almost no impulse control, rational thinking ability, empathy or social filter. To all intents he is telling you exactly what he thinks and focusing on what he wants to do, not what you want him to do. This is normal at this age.
>
> In terms of the listening, I would first stop and ask yourself if your communication is effective and if you are considering his feelings. For instance, are you asking him to do or, indeed, not do something when he is engrossed in an activity. If so, you will need to ask him several times and give him time to assimilate what you are saying. If you are taking him away from something else that he has far more interest in, then you need to show him as much empathy as possible:

'You are really busy with that jigsaw. I'm sorry to take you away from it.' Always focus on what it is you want him to do, not what you don't want him to do, and speak in short, clear sentences with only one command at a time. Understand though that he is only three, and it will be hard for him to focus on what you're saying, especially if something else has caught his attention.

When it comes to his shouting, this is likely to be a combination of learned behaviour, a stress response and a lack of impulse control. Learned behaviour means that he has likely learned the shouting from somewhere; unfortunately, the main source of this is usually parents, so I would look at whether you do sometimes lose your cool and shout at him or perhaps other members of the family. If we yell as parents, all we do is teach our children to yell too. Similarly, if you are asking him to do (or not do) something, and he is involved in another activity, or if it is something he really doesn't want to do, you could make him feel stressed. His response will be heightened if you repeat yourself several times, particularly if you start to lose your cool. This will put him into fight-or-flight mode and the shouting is a result of the adrenaline in his body readying him to fight. It is also indicative of an immature brain (normal for this age) and an inability to filter responses in a way that considers the feelings of others. As adults, we use our filter to present a more reasoned response. Your son doesn't have this yet and actually won't have for several years.

If you communicate carefully, understand what he is capable of and consider his feelings more, you may find that his behaviour is easier to deal with. When you ask him to do something, make sure you always empathise with him – 'I can see you were enjoying running and it's made you sad I've asked you to stop, hasn't it?' – then offer to help him to complete the task and also to calm down. Remember you are modelling all of the time though. When he shouts you could say, 'Ow, that hurt my ears. Let's speak quietly to each other.' Lastly, try to help your son to have a little more control over his life, give him more choices and more opportunities to make decisions – at the moment it sounds very much like his shouting is because he feels powerless. With fewer feelings of powerlessness, he will have less need to shout to try to feel more in control.

Q: *My eldest has just turned five. She is generally a very sensible child and, until recently, she has always listened to us when we've asked her not to do something. She is a sensitive child too and takes lots to heart.*

However, lately she has been very argumentative and really pushing the boundaries in certain situations, lashing out at her sister when she isn't 'first' or getting her own way, or if she feels her sister isn't listening to her. We are very much gentle parents, but her behaviour is causing my husband to question if we should be punishing her. She also seems to have become even more sensitive, complaining of bad dreams, constantly asking about death and accusing us of lying or not believing her. She started preschool at three with no issues, and is now at school with no issues, when she's there, that is; at home it's another story.

A: It sounds to me that your daughter is a very unhappy little girl right now. I think first of all you need to find the cause of her discomfort. You mention that she is fine at school, but not at home. This is an indication to me that she may be struggling at school. I know this may seem illogical, since she behaves well when she is there. However, children often work hard to keep it all together at school and then finally let everything out when they get home. For this reason, I would be having a chat with her teacher to ask about anything she may be struggling with, including peer relationships, schoolwork or something in the environment – often schools can be very overwhelming for little children with all the hustle and bustle. Next, you mention she has a sister, so I expect there is a degree of sibling rivalry here, especially if her sister is younger than her, so you should really focus on your relationship with her away from her sister: lots of one-to-one time alone just the two of you, outside the house, if possible.

The sensitivity is in part quite normal at this age, particularly worries about death. As children get older they lose the illusion of their world being a wonderful and safe place. Hearing something that has happened on the news about terrorism or murder, a death in the family or that of a pet or even talking about it at school can be very traumatic for young children. Also, as they get older, they begin to see flaws in their parents that they didn't see before and this can prove very unsettling to them. When you say she accuses you of not believing her, or lying to her, this makes me think you may need to work on your communication with her – listening to her in particular. Make sure that you don't try to dismiss her feelings, however far-fetched they may seem to you. If she is worried about something, then it is important to her and the worst thing you can do is say something like, 'Don't be silly', or, 'Stop worrying'. Taking some time to really listen to her concerns can help her to feel validated (even if you don't validate the actual concern). I would schedule in a bedtime chat every night for at least ten minutes, just the two of you, and ask her what the best and worst parts of her day have been. Then ask if she's worried about anything, every single night. Initially, it may be tricky if she is not used to opening up to you, but over time, hopefully, she will feel more comfortable.

To a degree, it is a child's role to push boundaries, but

the fact she is doing this a lot indicates to me that she needs more control in her life. If children feel powerless, they can often act in ways we really dislike, rudeness being one of them, to try to get some control. Ask her to help you choose boundaries and solutions to some common problems that you may experience and also allow her as much control as possible around things like free time, food, clothing and even room décor.

Empathy and listening, reconnection with you (without her sister around) and giving her more control should generate a big change in her behaviour. In your situation, I would say punishment is the worst approach you could take – it will turn a little girl who is unhappy into one who is very unhappy, but who feels incapable of communicating how she feels to you, which will set you up with all sorts of problems over the coming years. Focusing on your relationship with her now is key to preventing these problems that so many experience with tweens and teens.

Rudeness and backchat can be a real trigger for parents. It can often seem as if all your attempts to be compassionate and respectful have been thrown back in your face. Understanding that these behaviours are developmentally normal can go a long way towards reducing these feelings. Uncovering the underlying emotions and working with them using gentle-discipline methods may not stop the behaviour completely but, in time, you should notice a significant reduction.

Chapter 10

Coping with Sibling Rivalry

Do you have any brothers or sisters? Do you remember what your relationship with them was like growing up? Do you have any memories of feeling jealous of them, that your parents treated you differently in some way or that they were always in your space, playing with your toys and touching your belongings?

As parents, when we welcome another child into our family, we do so with thoughts of our child having a lifelong friend and companion – somebody who will be there for them after we pass away. We know that we love our children the same and have enough love to go around. They, however, may not share our view, at least not in the present.

How to deal with sibling arguments and fights often tops the list of questions I am asked by parents, whether it's a toddler struggling with the arrival of a new baby brother or sister or teenagers bickering over belongings, bedrooms and different treatment. Siblings may become firm friends as they enter adulthood, but in childhood things can be very different.

Perhaps the most common time for parents to experience sibling rivalry is the first few months, or years, following the arrival of a new baby. To begin with, your firstborn may be fascinated by their new brother or sister and excited by their arrival. As time goes on, however, they often find the adjustment difficult. Regression in sleeping, potty training and speech are common, as are increased tantrums and violent behaviour towards the baby. Parents often react to this by punishing the older child for being 'naughty' or jealous, with little regard to how they are feeling.

Why do most children struggle so much with the arrival of a new sibling? The easiest way to understand this is to think about how you would feel in a similar situation. Imagine the following scenario: you have been with your partner for several years; you love each other to bits and you have a really strong relationship. You have been out for the day and when you come home your partner introduces you to somebody you have never met before, saying: 'Hello, darling. How was your day? This is my new partner. I love them very much and I think the two of you are going to be great friends.' You start to protest, but they say, 'It's OK, I have enough love for the both of you. I love you just as much as I ever did, you're so special to me, but I love my new partner too. I think you will come to really love each other too.' How would you feel? I'm guessing you might be confused, angry, sad, let down. You might wonder why you weren't enough for your partner. You might protest and try to grab their attention away from their new partner. Perhaps you would insult the new partner and take all of your anger out on them. These are all the common and normal feelings often experienced by children who have just become a new big brother or sister.

There is also an argument that this behaviour is natural and primitive. Young mammals in the wild would die of hunger if they didn't let their parents know they were there. Similarly, it's as if a toddler with a new sibling is saying, 'I'm here. Look at me. Don't leave me!' When you think of it this way, it's quite clever – almost like a survival instinct.

Although these feelings can last for months or even years after the arrival of a new sibling, they are not the only cause of rivalry. Let's look at some of the other reasons.

Why siblings fight

Reducing sibling rivalry depends very much on understanding why it is happening. If you have warring siblings, or children who struggle around each other, the chances are that one, or more, of the common triggers outlined below are at work.

Lack of individual attention

Trying to give each child individual attention is difficult, especially if you work. Very often, families will do as much as possible together, largely in order to fit everything in to the hours in a day. Baths, bedtime routines, playtime, shopping trips, leisure time and dinner time are often done as a family. A lack of individual attention can, however, be a major trigger for undesirable behaviour, largely because the child feels a disconnect with you. Their connection with you can be damaged by a lack of individual time with them, but also made worse when they see you spending time with their sibling(s) and not with them.

When a new baby arrives, parents often adjust by dividing the labour so that the father takes care of the older child and the mother takes care of the baby. This is even more true if the mother is breastfeeding. Often, Dad will take the older child to day care or school or to the park, leaving Mum and the baby in peace. This separation of care often only adds to the problem, for it is not just their dad that the older sibling needs to spend one-to-one time with, but their mum too. Despite the good intentions, Dad taking almost sole charge of the older child makes them feel even more disconnected from their mother. This feeling can be directly linked with the love that they presume she has for them and it can be a source of great pain and sorrow. And how do 'wounded' children react? Often, they act out in undesirable ways with difficult behaviour.

In this situation, Dad needs to take care of the baby as much as possible, so that Mum can have time alone with her older child.

Comparisons

Comparing one child to another, particularly in a negative way, can really dent the relationship between children. Saying things like, 'See, your brother does what he's asked. Why can't you?' or, 'Your sister works really hard at school and does really well, but you just do really badly', can not only cause the child to feel a disconnect with you, but also lead to resentment of their 'better' sibling too. This commonly ends in arguments and fights. If you want to protect the sibling relationship, steer well clear of comparing your children, particularly in their presence.

Labelling

In families, labelling is rife. Parents often refer to children as 'the easy one', 'the clever one' or 'the naughty one', or use phrases such as, 'Oh, he's a handful', or, 'She's much harder work than her sister ever was.' Labelling is a problem for two reasons, the first being your subconscious expectations and the second being the growth of a fixed mindset: the more children are labelled by us as parents, the more we subconsciously treat them in ways that make the labelled behaviour more likely to occur. Perceiving one child as more difficult than the other can actually have a big influence on the way that you interact with the two of them. From the child's point of view, being viewed as the high-maintenance, needy or naughty sibling can lead them to believe that that is who they are and who they will always be. Of course, this isn't true – at any point they, and you, have the ability to change. But fulfilling this definition can become their role in your family, even if it is not a good one. This labelling can be very problematic indeed if one child is labelled 'good' and their sibling 'bad'. The rivalry this creates on both sides can be quite intense, with both children vying for a certain role.

Favouritism

If you have more than one child, do you have a favourite? Or perhaps a favourite on any given day? I certainly find one or two of my children are easier to handle at any particular time. Each day it changes and although the child who is the kindest and easiest at the time isn't my favourite, I am guilty of being nicer to them than I am to their siblings. Even without realising, we often treat our children differently, perhaps because they are our oldest, or our youngest, the same gender as us, or simply just easier. Although we may not mean to treat our children differently, we often do – and when we do, the child who is not treated so favourably may feel unloved and unappreciated. These feelings can serve to worsen their behaviour, often as they try to seek approval and attention from you.

Even if there is no favouritism, children can still feel as if they are second in your affections. Having the smallest bedroom, not being able to go to a club because their sibling has a sports practice that day and receiving hand-me-down clothing and toys can all leave children feeling as if you prefer their sibling over them, which can negatively affect both their behaviour and their relationship with their sibling.

Too much pressure on the eldest child

Very often I hear parents saying things like, 'You're three years older than him, start acting like it', or, 'Come on, you're the grown-up here, please just do what she's asked.' Sometimes, parents ask older siblings to keep an eye on their younger siblings – in some cases they don't want the extra responsibility; in others the job is so welcomed that they continue with it long after you have asked them to. Many older siblings can become bossy towards their younger siblings and attempt to discipline them, in a sense acting as their parent, rather than their brother or sister. Understandably, the younger siblings may not appreciate this. Plus, the older child might also think that certain rules do not apply to them, or that they have the right to take charge of the younger siblings, making it harder for you to discipline them. An imbalance of power between siblings can lead to many problems and hostility between them.

Too few opportunities to resolve their own problems

Far too many parents act as judge and jury when it comes to solving sibling arguments, but is this really good discipline? Think about what you want your children to learn from your discipline when they fight. Do you want them to learn to resolve problems amicably between themselves without needing your input? If so, then you must start from this position and help them to do it. The more you intervene, split them up, take a toy away, distract or admonish them, the less chance there is that they will learn how to resolve their differences. This lack of autonomy becomes a further trigger for sibling rivalry as children are then incapable of handling friction and problem solving in a calm and considerate way – a skill that will become vital as they grow up. This can quickly lead to more bickering, shouting and violent behaviour between siblings.

Reducing sibling rivalry

Once you have identified the 'Why?' and the 'How?', you can move on to the 'What?' – what do you want your children to learn from your discipline? Let's look at ways to handle specific issues.

More individual attention

First and foremost, ensure that each child gets as much individual attention from you as possible. You cannot move on to anything else until this is addressed. Children who do not have this need met will continue to behave in ways that are undesirable for two reasons: first, because they feel bad and sometimes unloved, and second, because, as far as they are concerned, any attention from you – even negative – is better than none. Quite simply, a child who seeks attention is a child who needs attention. And the best solution is to give it. It really is that straightforward.

So how do you manage to spend time with each child individually when you have more than one? I am asked this question every week. And the answer is, you make time. If you don't make time for individual attention, you will have to make time to handle difficult behaviour – and I know which I'd rather do. The easiest combination is probably a baby and an older child: when the baby naps, instead of rushing to clean and cook, you can play with your older child. Help them to understand that this is a time for just the two of you, and if they get upset during the day when the baby is awake, remind them that your special time is soon coming. When it comes around, just get on the floor with them and play, whatever they want to play. This is connection in the world of a child.

Finding time to reconnect with slightly older children can be harder. Bedtime is perhaps a good place to start. I always suggest that bedtime routines – including bath and story time – are never shared. If you have a partner with you, you have two choices: do bedtime routines for each child separately, while your partner watches the other child (or children); or, if the timings don't work for you, alternate each night, so that one night your partner does the bedtime routine for one child, while you do the other, then vice versa the next night. You may not get one-to-one time with both children every day, but at least you'll get it every other day.

If you don't have a partner or help in the evenings, you need to seek connection time during the day. Try to spend time with each child individually on a day-to-day basis; if you can do this out of the house, even for thirty minutes, so much the better. If you can't do it daily, think weekly. When my first two children were smaller and both at home all day, I employed a childminder every Tuesday for six hours – for my firstborn one week and the baby the next week. This gave me almost a full day every other week with each child, just the two of us. On a more infrequent basis, I try to spend a day or night, or a weekend, with each of my four children in turn. This is our special time. The child picks (within reason) the activity and the two of us spend time alone together doing something they really want to do. We have done concerts, shopping trips and theatre shows. Sometimes, I have to travel with my work (when I am on a book tour, speaking at conferences, or running workshops), and I always try to take one of my children with me, so that they get to spend a longer period alone with me. These trips really help us to reconnect and there is a significant improvement in their behaviour for quite a long time when we return home.

The more your child is misbehaving and the worse the sibling rivalry is, the more you should spend time with them individually. If the fighting is at extreme levels and funds stretch to even the cheapest bed-and-breakfast accommodation, a night and day away for just you and one of your children is in order. Take the most challenging child first and explain to the other that you are taking their sibling away to help them to calm down and reduce their fights. When you have time and funds available again take the other child and explain the same to their sibling. Of course, you don't have to spend money in order to spend more time with your children. It may be possible to home swap with a relative, whereby you stay at their home with the child who is in need of more one-to-one time and they stay at yours to look after your other children. Or perhaps you have a friend who would consider helping you with babysitting, so that you can have time alone with one child now and again and you return the favour at some point. Regardless of your financial or personal situation, there is always a way to achieve this most important time alone with your children – sometimes you just have to think outside the box a little and create your own opportunities.

Encourage co-operation and equality

In terms of equality, try not to label your children in any way. You don't have 'a quiet one', 'a loud one', 'a clever one' and 'a

naughty one'. You just have children with unique personalities – children who hopefully know that they can change their
behaviour whenever they want. Try your hardest not to treat
them differently when it comes to discipline. For instance,
don't let your youngest get away with more than your eldest
does (or did at the same age). And avoid giving any power, or
heaping expectations onto your eldest – phrases such as, 'You're
older, you should know better', or, 'You're the grown-up one
here, just let her have it' – and don't ever ask your eldest to
assume responsibility for disciplining their younger siblings.

Treating children equally is so important when it comes to
fostering co-operation. You can further encourage their co-
operation skills by investing in some games – usually board
games – where the children work together to win, and there are
no individual winners or losers (see page 268). Also encourage
your children to engage in as many team-type tasks and activities as possible, such as cleaning the car as a team or creating
a quiz together for you to answer.

Encourage child–based problem solving

Your children need to learn how to resolve conflict themselves,
ideally without your input, so it is really important that you
don't take sides or take over. When you see them fighting or one
of them complains to you, respond in a way that encourages
them to solve their own problems. Your side of the conversation
might be something like this:

Hey, I can see two very unhappy children here. What's
going on?
   *At this point, if they both try to speak at the same time, you
say*: Whoa, I can't hear. Child A – tell me what happened?
   Now, Child B, tell me what happened?

Child A, how did it make you feel? How do you think B felt?

B, how did it make *you* feel? And how do you think A felt?

A, can you think of a way to resolve this, so that you're both happy?

B, can *you* think of a way to resolve this, so you're both happy?

Hmm, that sounds really good, but I'm not so sure you'll both be happy? Who can think of a solution that you're both OK with? *At this point, hopefully, the children will come up with something; if not, you can prompt a little.*

Wow, that sounds like a great solution to me! I'm really proud that you can both decide on some good solutions.

Initially, you will have to prompt them lots to gently tease out their problem-solving skills, but with time you will find that they begin to resolve any issues without adult input. You may have to repeat this process many, many times, but each time you do, your child will learn something and, eventually, there will come a time where you will hear them begin to argue and then work through the process alone. That is a wonderful moment indeed!

Create private spaces

Children can squabble because they feel that their personal space has been invaded or that their siblings are touching things that belong to them without their permission. To make things worse, many don't have their own private space to retreat to when this happens, so that they can calm down. If you are a parent of squabbling siblings, try to ensure that each has their own space. In an ideal world, this would be their own bedroom, but otherwise their own section of your home is OK – say, a small corner of a room where they can keep their belongings and where they can go (alone) if needed. If you have a garden, I highly recommend giving each child an area to tend (no matter how small) – or even a plant pot each will suffice. Allow them to select what they will grow in their plot (or pot) and encourage them to tend to their own 'garden'.

Creating a private space is only part of the issue though. The next step is teaching your children to respect each other's spaces. Encourage door knocking and requesting to enter before they go into somebody's room. And you should afford them the same respect.

Real family case studies

As previously, when you read through the case studies below, see if you can identify the cause of the behaviour (the 'Why?'), understand how the child feels (the 'How?') and what a good discipline solution would be (the 'What?'). Sibling rivalry always contains a why and a how, usually very easy to spot – unless you are looking at your own family, when it can be trickier.

> **Q:** *I have an eleven-year-old daughter who is very rivalrous with her eight-year-old brother. It has always been like that, since the day he was born. He is a gentle boy, softly spoken and will never cause a fight. Everyone likes him. My daughter likes her other siblings and treats them well – all except for her youngest brother. I think perhaps he is the one who caused her to get less attention – or at least that is how I see it. She just doesn't back off and it is very upsetting to see her mistreat him this way.*

A: I think you have a couple of issues here.

The first is that your daughter is desperate for some individual attention from you. At the moment, I suspect that most of your attention towards her is quite negative – perhaps because you are constantly trying to get her to leave her brother alone. I would recommend, if possible, that you arrange a special day for just the two of you. Tell your daughter that you'd really like to spend some time with her and that you'd love to go somewhere for the day together. Ask if she has any ideas of where you can go and research and discuss them with her. Book a date, and, if you have a family calendar, mark it on there with a special star. Talk about it lots in the run-up. On the day, focus on really trying to bond with your daughter, and when you get home, tell her how much you have enjoyed the day and that you hope that you can do it again soon. Try to do something one-to-one with her every day too, even if it's just a fifteen-minute chat, sitting on the side of her bed before she goes to sleep at night. Don't view her need for your attention and her upset at having lost a lot of it to her brother as a negative thing. It isn't. In fact, you could almost see it as a compliment on your mothering skills and your daughter's sadness at having lost – in her view – some of your connection.

Next, I would recommend that you really work on your opinions and expectations of your children. It can be really easy to slip into a habit of labelling them according to their qualities (as you have done with your son). These expectations and labels can be very damaging in many ways. First, if your daughter hears you speaking about your son in a very positive way and her in a negative way, it can cause her a great deal of hurt and can make her behave in the way you describe. Think also about your actions towards them: are you harder on your daughter than your son? Do you blame her when it may, in fact, be his fault, only you are so used to it being hers? Your daughter has to feel that she is treated fairly by you. Having an 'easy' younger child, particularly the youngest in the family, can cause quite a lot of subconscious favouritism, which is reflected in our behaviour. I do wonder if your daughter may be picking up on this.

Q: *I have two boys, almost six and almost four respectively. They have totally different personalities, but both are very strong-willed and they clash! One has a very mathematical and logical mind and insists that everything has to be done 'right' – the rules in games must be followed, for example. The other is much more of a 'free spirit' – outgoing, haphazard, imaginative. They are very fond of each other fundamentally, but they also argue all the time. When one says they want to do something, the other has to do it too – even if they showed no interest in that thing thirty seconds earlier. If I ask one of them a question and they answer, the other will swear the answer is something different. It's almost like they have to compete just for the sake of it. And then there's the usual arguments over who sits where on the sofa, what they want to watch on TV, etc. How do we foster a more harmonious relationship? The constant bickering is exhausting.*

A: I would focus on getting your boys to work together as a team, pooling their strengths to create a wonderful force. If you don't have some already, I would suggest that you invest in some co-operative games (usually board games) that focus on winning as a team, not as individuals. Your boys can then work together to achieve, rather than playing off each other in a negative way. I would also urge you to involve them in other tasks that take account of both of their unique personalities. For instance, you could suggest they put on a play, with the more imaginative one being the actor and the logical one directing or creating a programme. You could encourage them to build models together, one focusing on the aesthetics and decoration, the other on the structural integrity. The more you support them in working as a team, but in an individual way, the better you will find that they fit together.

Next, I would also focus on getting some private space for each of them, perhaps their own rooms, or their own area of your living room, where they can engage in their own activities in privacy and away from each other when they need space. When it comes to choosing television programmes, work with them to see if they can come up with a solution – perhaps they could make their own television guide and block out an equal amount of time each, watching what they want to watch. I'm sure if you involve them, they will be able to come up with some creative solutions – again, between them it sounds as if they could do some great problem solving.

Q: *My daughter is almost three and my son is almost one. My daughter was always a very kind and gentle child, until her brother started crawling, that is. She is going through the developmental phase associated with her age (or I'm assuming she is): not wanting him taking her toys, wanting the toy he is playing with just because he has it, etc. The hardest thing is when, for example, I am in the kitchen and so is my son. He'll be happily playing and then my daughter will come in and deliberately hurt him (usually by pushing him over). You can see sometimes that he is frightened of her and it's so upsetting. No amount of kind and gentle approaches have helped. I've started to ask her if she would like him to do it back to her because that's how he learns, through copying. How do you deal with deliberate aggressive behaviour, particularly to a sibling?*

A: I can understand your daughter's frustration. She had a happy existence with you and your full attention for two years, then an imposter came along. He took 50 per cent of your attention away from her, if not more. And in a toddler's world, attention equals love. So, from your daughter's perspective, you have 50 per cent less love for her than you did a year ago. What does she need to reassure her that you do still love her and didn't have another child because she wasn't enough for you? The answer is: your time and attention. You are stuck in a never-ending cycle of her needing your attention and doing things that she knows will get it, such as hurting her brother. But the attention she gets isn't positive, so she feels bad and more disconnected which, in turn, makes her act in an even more unkind way towards her brother. He is the one who made everything change in her world, and although she may eventually have a great relationship with him, and fleeting moments of friendship now, she isn't in a place of appreciating him yet.

On top of this emotional turmoil, she can't even play in peace. Her brother takes her toys and touches the only things that are truly hers. Since she already has to share you, it is totally understandable that she doesn't want her brother to share her belongings too. I really feel for her.

You have two important steps to take. The first is to reassure her that you love her just as much as before and to give her as much positive attention as possible. The more time you can spend out of the house with her away from her brother the better (or vice versa, with somebody taking her brother out for the day). She needs time with you – regular time – just like it used to be a year ago. Spend time with her one-to-one, talking to her and reading a story to her in her bedroom every night (don't do bedtimes together) and, at the weekend, take her to the park, or perhaps swimming, leaving her brother with friends or family.

Next, you need to get her a private space away from her brother – a space he cannot go into unless she invites him; somewhere where he cannot touch her belongings or spoil her play. My best suggestion here would be to get a large playpen (you can get some that have fabric sides and a roof to make them like a little den) to be her secure sanctuary. When she wants to get away from her brother she can let herself in and close the door, safe in the knowledge that he can't get to her or her toys. Encourage her to put everything she really loves and doesn't want her brother to touch in the playpen and when you see her struggling, remind her to use it. Better still, you could go in there with her.

The suggestions and advice in this chapter are not quick fixes. Siblings will always fall out, not want to share, vie for your attention and, occasionally, disrespect each other's privacy and belongings. With plenty of thought, hard work and consistency, however, you can turn a tricky sibling relationship into a friendship that will last for life.

Chapter 11

Coping with Lying

Children who lie are often considered antisocial and lacking in morals, and parents can wonder what they did wrong to raise a dishonest child. Yet isn't it ironic that we expect our children to be honest when we lie so much ourselves?

Think back over the last week, for example – did you tell somebody that they looked good when they didn't? Did you bump into somebody and tell them how great it was to see them again, when actually you thought the opposite? Did you promise your child that you would do something 'later', or imply that you would consider buying something for Christmas or their birthday when you had no intention of doing so? Did you zone out when your partner was talking to you and answer, 'Yes, of course I am', when they asked if you were listening to them? Did you say, 'Thank you, it's lovely', when you received a gift that you disliked? Did you tell somebody, 'Let's catch up soon', when you had no wish to meet up with them again . . .

You may be thinking that these lies are told in order to avoid hurting people's feelings. And so they are. But this is one of the top reasons why children lie too – most of their lies are intended to make you and them feel better, and understanding this might change how you think about them.

Conventional parenting methods take a very hard line on lying. The child is labelled 'devious', 'deceptive', 'dishonest' and 'manipulative', the assumption being that lying always comes from a place of negativity and, as such, it almost always results in a punishment. In this chapter, however, we will look at things a little differently, bearing in mind that – in most cases – lying stems from a place of positivity. Knowing that your child is perhaps lying to spare your feelings is likely to dramatically change the way you discipline. So let's first look at the most common motivators for lying and how to deal with them in a gentle manner.

How we encourage lying as parents

As parents we unwittingly make our children lie on a daily basis. We phrase our questions to them in a manner that encourages them to lie: 'That wasn't you was it?'; 'I know you would never do anything like that'; 'You did do what I asked, didn't you?' These questions or statements suggest to the child how much trouble they will be in if they admit the truth, and push them to answer in the way you would like, which, in many cases, means lying.

Another way that we force our children to lie is by teaching them social niceties. However, each time we make them lie to appease others, we tell them that it is acceptable in order to keep people happy. Let's look at some examples.

All parents want to raise kind, polite and thoughtful children. So making them say they are sorry when they hurt someone is a given. Young children who hurt another physically or psychologically are expected to apologise; if they don't, they are considered rude and inconsiderate. Forcing younger children to say they are sorry, however, may lead to them growing up to be less kind and thoughtful and can encourage them to lie. Due to their underdeveloped Theory of Mind (see page 61), young children have a hard time understanding the viewpoint of others, which means that they naturally struggle with empathy. Empathy, as we learned right at the beginning of this book, is one of the last social skills to develop in children. While some children have distinctly better empathy skills than others, it is unreasonable to expect a reasonable amount until they start school.

You may be wondering why I am talking about empathy, when this chapter is about lying. Are the two related? The answer is yes, they absolutely are. Empathy implies that the child feels bad for what they have done, and in order to feel bad they have to understand how they have made another feel. For instance, if a toddler hits or bites another toddler at a playgroup, saying they are sorry would imply that they understood that the other child is in pain. It also implies that they regret hurting the other child and wish to make them feel better. If they have poor empathy skills (as is normal for this age), they will not have such train of thought. In fact, if they bit or hit another child in order to get hold of a toy that they wanted, they may believe that the injured child feels happy, as they themselves are happy now that they have the toy. Forcing the child to apologise in this instance does not make the child sorry; all it does is force them to lie.

Why children lie

Let's look at some of the other reasons why children lie so you can start to understand the 'Why?' and the 'How?' of lying.

Because they love you

Most parents of children who lie a lot think that they do so because they don't like or respect them. In most cases, however, the opposite is true. Children usually lie because they really love their parents and don't want to upset them. If a child admits to doing something that they know their parents will disapprove of, they often feel that they have let their parents down. They know that they will be sad, or angry, and so they lie to save their feelings.

Sometimes, children love their parents so much that they don't want to admit that they have done something wrong for fear that this will negatively affect their parents' feelings about them – they may lie to protect their relationship.

They have been trained to lie for fear of punishment

If your child tells the truth about something that they have done wrong, and you punish them in return, you are training them, through the process of conditioning, to be less likely to tell you the truth in the future.

When a child makes a mistake they need parents who will listen to and support them. You may not be proud of what your child has done, but when they admit their wrongdoings to you they have already been punished enough by their own conscience. They do not need to be made to feel even worse. No matter what your child confesses to you, you have to remain calm and focus on gentle discipline. Think about what you want them to learn and the best way to achieve that. Mostly the answer lies in discussion, teaching, coaching and helping them to understand a better way to behave in the future.

The minute that your child is brave enough to tell you the truth and you punish them, you drastically increase the likelihood that they will lie to you the next time they do something wrong.

They don't trust you with their truth

If you want your child to talk to you and tell you the truth, no matter how embarrassed or uncomfortable they may feel, you have to listen.

Listening intently, even when you don't feel like doing so, or when you don't consider what the child is talking about important, is the key to building good communication for the future. If you belittle, admonish or criticise their actions or feelings, you make it more likely that they will withhold or lie about them in the future.

Similarly, if your child confesses something to you, keep it secret between the two of you as far as possible. Sharing their actions and feelings with others when you don't need to will decrease their trust in you: if they think that you cannot keep something personal private, they are more likely to lie to you in the future.

Because they feel bad about the truth

Even as adults, we don't like to confess when we have said or done something wrong and we feel bad about our actions. Children are no different. If a child says or does something that they know is wrong, confessing means admitting their mistake out loud. This is a form of cognitive dissonance (see page 171). In many ways this is a protective mechanism. It stops them from having to cope with the negative feelings that they would otherwise have about themselves.

Peer pressure

As children get older the influence of their peers increases. They may feel forced into doing something in order to receive peer approval. Lying to parents about where they are going, or what they are doing, in order to avoid any negativity from their peers is not uncommon in the tween and, particularly, teen years. This effect increases if your boundaries are too strict or cause them difficulties with 'fitting in'.

How do you encourage children to be honest?

The answer here is quite simple. Don't make your children scared of telling you the truth, and don't encourage them to lie.

Help your child to understand that there is nothing in this world that they cannot tell you. When they confide in you, keep their confession private between the two of you as much as possible. Listen intently to what they are telling you, hold back on blame and punishment, stay calm and think about how you can support them. Once again remember the 'Why? How? What?' approach. Ask yourself why they are lying to you? Is it because they are scared of your reaction if they tell you the truth? Are they afraid of upsetting you? Then consider how they are feeling. In most cases, they will not be feeling good. If they have done something wrong, they are likely to feel anxious, scared, guilty and worried, and they will also be experiencing a degree of cognitive dissonance. Even though you may feel awful hearing their truth, never underestimate how bad they feel holding on to it. Lastly, think about what you want to achieve in terms of discipline. If you want them to tell you the truth in the future, you must work on your response to them – you must stay calm and help to guide them to a better response or better choices in the future.

When it comes to subconsciously encouraging them to lie, this requires a large degree of self-study. How often do you think you lie on an average day? Is there a way that you can reduce your insincerity to set a better example for your child to follow? Think too about your requests for them to lie to appease other people. Is what you are asking really necessary? Is there a better way that you could approach the situation that would keep all parties happy, but not encourage your child to lie?

My story

I would like to end this chapter with a scenario that happened in my own family when my daughter was five years old, and a description of how I handled it. As I talk you through it, try to pick out the 'Why?', the 'How?' and the 'What?' in my story.

My daughter is spirited, clever and funny and we have an exceptionally strong bond, but when she was very young she tended to lie an awful lot. One day, I had bought my son a new chest of drawers for his bedroom. It was very large and heavy and we needed help to manoeuvre it up our small, winding stair-case. While we waited for a friend to help, the chest of drawers remained in our entrance hall for a couple of days. When some large black dots appeared on the drawers, looking very much like they had been made with my large permanent black marker pen, I asked my sons who had made the marks and they all said, individually, that it was their sister. I also had my own suspicions as to the culprit, due to the rather immature-looking marks and my daughter's then obsession with drawing on everything. The boys confirmed my thoughts and I was certain it was her.

My daughter, however, was not forthcoming with the truth. I asked, calmly, if it was her and she replied, 'It wasn't me', before crying and storming out of the room in a sulk. I left it, hoping she would come back and confess to me, but she didn't. Twenty minutes later, I found her curled up on the sofa in the playroom looking very sorry for herself. I asked her again if she had made the marks and reminded her that lying to me was always worse than telling the truth, whatever it was that she had done. I told her that she had nothing to fear by telling me the truth, but she refused to talk to me. I asked her to take some time to consider whether she would like to talk to me and tell me what she had done. I also suggested that she might like to help me to clean the marks off.

Another ten minutes went by, then she came quietly into the room where I was, sobbing, saying, 'Mummy, you hurt my feelings.' I asked if she would like a hug. She didn't reply. Instead, she climbed onto my lap, pulled me close and buried her head in my arms, still crying. I hugged her back and told her I loved her. Once she had calmed down I asked her if she would like to tell me anything. 'I'm sorry,' she whispered. 'Would you like to help me clean the marks off?' I asked. Slowly, she nodded, tears rolling down her cheeks. I said, 'I know you know that you shouldn't have drawn on the drawers.' She nodded. I then said, 'Thank you for telling me the truth.' We hugged for a long time before cleaning the drawers together.

That wasn't the only time she lied, and the same is likely to be true for your child when you adopt a more gentle approach, but my method remains the same to this day. Each time, I hope I instil a little of the importance of telling the truth and help her to trust that she can tell me anything, no matter what it is, and I will always treat her calmly and kindly and help her to resolve the situation.

*

Although this chapter has given you some hints and tips on how to handle and decrease lying, I think it is important to understand that we all, every single one of us, lie. Lying, as we've seen, is not always negative – sometimes, the motivation is incredibly altruistic. It is likely that your child will continue to lie at times, but your main goal here is to foster a relationship with them in which they always feel safe enough to tell you their truth. This may not be what you want to hear, but, no matter what they tell you, you must respond from a position of calmness, respect and support. Ultimately, our real goal as parents is to raise children who feel able to tell us anything and always come to us for help.

Chapter 12

Coping with Swearing

The first time your child swears, particularly if it is in public, will be one of the most mortifying experiences of parenthood. There is an unspoken assumption that children who swear are badly brought up, but swearing in children is entirely normal and very common, no matter how they are parented. Gently disciplined children are no exception.

Many years ago, I was at a craft event, looking at some wood carvings, when my son shouted 'Fuck off' to his brother, incredibly loudly. I am not exaggerating when I say that every single person around us turned to stare at him and, in turn, at me. I could imagine what they were thinking: 'Can't she control her child?' and 'What an awful family – the parents must speak like that to the children; they must have learned it from somewhere.' I wanted the ground to open up and swallow me.

In that instance, my son was angry that his brother kept on bumping into him; he was tired, it was hot, he was thirsty and he just snapped. Just as we all do at times. I have also had experiences of my children swearing when they were much younger. When my daughter was four years old and in reception class at school, I was called to speak to the teacher at the end of the day.

She blushed as she told me my daughter had kept repeating the word 'fuck' all afternoon. I still don't know where she learned it, but that evening we had to have a big talk about why it was inappropriate to say it, especially at school.

My children are still prone to 'blowing up' occasionally, and now they are all tweens and teens, swear words feature fairly regularly in their vocabulary, as is the case with most young people. Adults too tend to swear, and this can be for one, or all, of three reasons. First, because they enjoy it; second, because they struggle to control their anger and react in a more appropriate way; and, lastly, because they have learned it from their own childhood or peers. Things are not very different for children.

Why do children swear?

Sometimes, there are very clear triggers for swearing; other times, you will be utterly flummoxed as to the reason. If there are triggers, however, you are not going to resolve the swearing until you deal with them.

Let's look at the most common reasons why children swear. As we go through this section, keep in mind the 'Why? How? What?' framework: why is your child swearing? How are they feeling? And what do you hope to achieve from your discipline?

The fight-or-flight response

This tops the list as a reason why we all swear, no matter how old we are. When we are stressed or scared, our bodies are flooded with adrenaline and we are primed to fight or run from whatever is threatening us. For adults, the potential causes of stress are numerous – it may be road rage, following an altercation with an incompetent driver, or perhaps you have spent hours preparing a special dish and you drop it as you take it out of the oven, or you may be running late for an important meeting and then you can't find your car keys. In these situations, and others like them, swearing is common, no matter how well-spoken we may be when we are calm.

Children experience the same effect. They may not be worrying about driving, baking or meetings, but this doesn't mean that they do not have triggers. Suddenly realising, ten minutes before they leave for school, that they have homework due in, losing something that a friend has lent them, fighting with their siblings and desperately wanting to play when you are insisting that they tidy their room can all be triggers. In all of these cases, adult or child, the body's survival instinct activates the part of the brain responsible for surviving, not thinking. Swearing is a common response – it is almost a way for the brain to calm down and restore equilibrium.

Lack of impulse control

This is what heightens the fight-or-flight response even more in children. When we are stressed, particularly in the company of others, or in locations where calm and professional behaviour is expected, we have the ability to override our need to shout 'Oh, shit' at the top of our lungs. Children don't, even if they are teenagers. We have previously learned that impulse control doesn't develop fully until we enter our twenties, so whether your child is three or thirteen their ability to restrain themselves is going to be pretty poor. To a child, it doesn't matter where they are or who they are with – if they find themselves in a situation where they have a strong desire to swear, there is little they can do to stop it.

Learned behaviour

Speaking in hushed tones, spelling out words instead of speaking them, or quickly glancing to see if they are watching and listening to you are not effective ways to reduce the impact of your swearing on your children. Similarly, telling your child, 'I don't expect you to repeat what I have just said', has little or no influence. Quite simply, if you swear, your child will do the same.

As with Bandura's experiment on modelling aggression (see page 29), children model what they say on what they hear from us. They are always listening to what you say, even if you think they are not. So, if you don't want your child to swear, there is only one solution: you must stop swearing too.

Power struggles and lack of attention

As we have seen throughout this book, if children feel powerless, they will try to gain some control via their behaviour, and swearing is a wonderful way for them to do this: they instantly grab your attention and the ball is in their court – they control what happens next, whether they swear again, or stop.

If your child is going through a particularly testing period of increased swearing, this is a strong indication that you need to give them more power over their own lives and within the family. Encourage them to make more decisions for the family and become as involved as possible. From an attention perspective, make sure that you have plenty of one-to-one time with them and really listen to them if they are trying to talk to you, or if their behaviour is indicating that something is wrong.

Testing words and phrases for effect

This is similar to the previous point about attention, but the motivation is slightly different. It is more common in younger children whose 'job' is all about testing boundaries and learning their place in the world. They test the effects of what they say on those around them, perhaps because they have been in a situation where they observed another child swearing and receiving a big response from adults. This type of swearing doesn't necessarily mean that the child has any underlying trauma or big feelings; it is simply experimentation and observation.

Liking how the words feel – or lacking alternatives

Have you ever noticed how good it feels to say certain swear words? They are often 'big' sounds and quite lyrical and even musical. They usually start and end with strong-sounding consonants and are mostly only one or two syllables long. Simply put, they sound good and feel good to form in your mouth. So sometimes, children choose a swear word because they cannot think of another one to appropriately describe their feelings; other times, they swear simply because they like how the word sounds. Once again, there is no malice or manipulation here and, often, no uncomfortable feelings underpinning the swearing.

How should you respond to swearing?

As with all discipline, your reaction should be based on asking yourself why your child is acting in this way: uncover the motivation and you will find the most appropriate response. Let's look at some of the most common techniques to help to diminish swearing.

Don't ignore it

The most common advice concerning swearing in children is to just ignore it and they will stop eventually, or not to react, as they are only doing it for that reason. This is bad advice.

Ignoring swearing totally misses addressing the cause – and if you do not remove the cause, you can only palliate, but you won't make the underlying issues go away. They will reappear in a different guise, or just farther down the line. If you ignore your child's swearing, they may learn that there is no point in swearing around you as you don't respond. However, they might swear in front of other people, as they may well react. The reason behind the swearing doesn't go away; they just learn not to bother with you and thus seek out others to swear at.

Don't overreact

The more you overreact, and go crazy in response to your child's swearing, the more they are likely to do it. Why? Because they have power over you – they can make you act that way, just by saying one or two little words. Can you imagine what it feels like to a child to have so much control over somebody?

To avoid this, always stay calm, keep your voice at normal volume and reply in a matter-of-fact way. This helps your child to learn that they cannot control you by swearing, which, in turn, lessens its appeal somewhat. It also helps to be human: admit to your child that you also swear some-times, and that's OK because nobody is perfect, but that you try to keep it to a minimum and not to swear outside the house because it offends people and may make them think badly of you.

Explain what the words mean

The two 'it' words at our local secondary school at the moment seem to be 'retard' and 'twat', and my two oldest boys suddenly started saying each of them regularly. They are not words we use at home and it is obvious that they picked them up at school. Hearing them for a second or third time I asked my sons to come and sit with me, and asked them if they knew what the words meant? They replied, 'A twat is a stupid person', to which I said: 'No, it is a slang word for a vagina.' I asked them if they would feel comfortable calling people 'vagina'. They giggled and said, 'Of course not!' 'So why is twat OK, now you know what it means?' I asked. I suggested that the next time their friends use the word they could ask them if they know what the word means and, between them, decide if they really want to carry on using it. Since our discussion and their new understanding of the meaning of the word, their use of it has dramatically lessened.

In some cases, children have a vague idea of what a word means, but don't really understand the implications of saying it. The use of the word 'retard' by my children and their friends definitely fits into this category. Once again, we had a discussion about the word 'retard' and how it was incredibly offensive. This led on to a conversation about various syndromes and the genetic basis behind them and how everybody should be treated as an individual, regardless of their disabilities. I asked my sons if they would speak to somebody with learning difficulties and call them a retard to their face, knowing what they now knew. Of course, they said they wouldn't. I then asked, why they thought it was OK to use the word for others, particularly now that they knew what it meant – so not only was it incredibly insulting to those living with certain conditions, it was also incorrect in the case of others. Once again, their use of the word has drastically diminished. When I hear them use it, we have another talk about how other people feel and why it is important to be respectful. Hopefully, this will ultimately have a much stronger effect on them than the peer pressure to use the words.

Fulfil their need for power and attention

If your child is swearing because they are desperately trying to attract your attention, the answer is simple. Give them more attention and you remove that need.

From a power perspective, you should provide your child with more opportunity to be in control: ask them to choose dinner for the whole family, select a television programme for everyone to watch or decide what you will do at the coming weekend. Set aside time when you interact with them – conversations, cuddles or play every day – so that they know that they always have a set time when you are effectively under their control.

Focus on the emotion behind the words

If your child is shouting and swearing at you, or someone else, ignore the specific word, but respond to the emotion that is triggering their behaviour: 'You seem really angry right now, can I help?', or, 'You seem really upset about something, can you tell me about it?' This way, the behaviour, or the cause of the swearing, is validated and heard and you can work together to find a more appropriate and effective way to handle the emotions. At this point, the swearing is not necessary any more; you have removed the need for it and it stops naturally.

Provide an acceptable alternative

When your child is very worked up, particularly in fight-or-flight mode, when they have less cognitive ability and a lack of impulse control, try to find alternative words for them to use. These should be discussed and agreed when the child is calm and, ideally, they should choose the words. Encourage a brainstorming session when you can come up with other words – the sillier the better, and as similar as possible to the swear word they most commonly use in terms of sound and syllables. Ideally, the words will be made up, to give the child ownership – for example, 'bipp' for 'shit' or 'wuf uff' for 'fuck off'. Remind your child of their alternative words if they forget them in the heat of the moment.

Real family case studies

Let's end with the experiences of some real parents. As I answer their questions, think back to the causes of swearing that we discussed at the start of this chapter and see if you can work out why the child is swearing (the 'Why?'), an understanding of how the child feels (the 'How?') and what a good discipline solution would be (the 'What?').

> Q: *My twelve-year-old shouts and swears a lot if he doesn't get his own way. He is also a nightmare in the morning before school, when I'm trying to get him ready and he will often swear at me. I've been trying to ignore it for quite a long time now, but it's not getting any better.*

> A: I think there are a couple of things happening here. First, it sounds as if your son is really struggling with feeling powerless. This is common at this age, as he straddles childhood and adulthood, and boundaries can be harder to accept, particularly if he sees you breaching your own rules. Try to understand how he feels when you are in control of most elements of his life and he has little choice but to follow your orders. Now and again it would be good to let him 'get his own way' if there are any boundaries you are happy to relax a little. Try other ways to help him feel he has a little more power too. For instance, if the fight is over you saying he should clean his room, ask if he can suggest ways to make his room easier to tidy – by introducing a bin or storage boxes under his bed, for example. And ask if he can think of a solution that could make both of you happy, the end result being a tidy room, but the two of you getting along and both feeling as if your requests and needs have been considered. I would also recommend that you spend some time really trying to make friends with your son – this can be such a tricky age when it comes to fights and disagreements and this unspoken warring can continue for many days, weeks or months. If you can, try to spend a day with just the two of you doing something fun together; ask

your son to pick what you do, and try as hard as you can not to nag him or tell him off all day. Make sure you tell him what fun you're having and how you really love it when you get on so well with him; tell him you miss his company and you'd love to try to reduce the fights at home.

Next, it also sounds as if your son is struggling with time management and organisation. Again, this is so common at this age. Tweens and teens excel at disorganisation and oversleeping. It is simply biological. Try working with your son to help him organise his mornings and school preparations – things like getting his bag packed and his shoes and uniform ready in a safe place the night before, so that he knows where everything is. And give yourself extra time in the morning, so that there isn't a last-minute panic just before you leave the house. Empathise with him as well – 'Mornings are tough, aren't they? I struggle too' – so you are not directly responding to the bad language, but to the underlying emotions.

Q: *Our wonderful son is three years old and over the last month or two his love for swear words, particularly 'bugger', has reached crisis point. Most days now it seems to be the first thing he says in the morning. He even tells me it's his favourite word! We don't know how to deal with it; nothing has worked. Gentle ideas needed, desperately! I don't know how many more times I can handle hearing his 'Hi, you bugger!' to random strangers in the supermarket ...*

A: I think one of two things (or possibly both) is happening here, the first being that your son, as he says, simply likes the word. Bugger is actually a really nice word to say linguistically. It sounds quite amusing and the combination of the 'b' and hard 'g's feels good on your lips and in your mouth. I can understand the appeal. It is also very similar to the word 'bug', and identifying and catching creepy crawlies is usually high up on a preschooler's list of favourite pastimes.

Next, you say nothing has worked, which leads me to think you have tried several things, perhaps totally ignoring him or overreacting a little. Most people respond to swearing in a way that gives the child great glee, because they have so much power from using just one little word. This is heightened if your son feels he doesn't have much control over his life, or that he doesn't get as much attention as he'd like, perhaps because you're busy working or looking after another child. The best thing is not to ignore him, but to respond in a very matter-of-fact way that neither excites nor discounts him.

If he were a little older I would suggest explaining to him the meaning of the word 'bugger' and why it is inappropriate for him to use it. For now, however, I would have a conversation with him when he is calm, and tell him that lots of people don't like the word, and that when he is outside the home he will need to use an alternative. Ask him to come up with a word that is similar in length, syllables and sound – ideally, made up and as silly as possible. For instance, flugger, brubber or fligger. When he next says the word, you instantly reply: 'No. It's flugger/brubber/ fligger – remember?' Turn it into a bit of a game, laughing and challenging him to get the word 'right'.

Lastly, don't expect a quick change. You will need to do all of this for probably two months, maybe more, but if you are consistent with the approach, you will see a change.

There are no quick fixes for stopping swearing. Often, the causes are multiple and, given the correlation between swearing and the development of impulse control and stress management in particular, it can take a long time to change. You may well need to repeat the techniques suggested here many times. In the meantime, remind yourself that the swearing is not your fault; it is common and normal, so try not to take it personally. You are not a bad parent, even if your child swears in the middle of a shopping centre. It happens to everybody at some point. That's not to say that you should just accept it, and I hope that this chapter has given you plenty of tips to help reduce, if not stop, the swearing.

Chapter 13

Coping with Low Self-esteem and a Lack of Confidence

You may be wondering why there is a chapter on low self-esteem and a lack of confidence in a book about discipline and coping with difficult behaviour. Why would you want to discipline your child for having low self-esteem?

In fact, it is very important to consider these issues because often they underpin difficult behaviour. So how might a lack of self-esteem or confidence manifest in terms of undesirable behaviour? Here are just a few examples – the list is by no means complete:

- Whining – trying to get parental attention because they feel bad and are, therefore, more needy.

- Sulking – feeling that the world is against them and that they will never be good enough.

- Violent behaviour – externalising the uncomfortable feelings that they have and blaming others for not feeling good.

- Difficult behaviour at school – particularly as an attempt to override a lack of confidence in their academic abilities.

- Swearing and backchat – to cover up feelings of vulnerability.

- Ignoring your requests to do certain things – sometimes because they doubt their ability, so would rather save face and refuse to do them in the first place.

- Being bad losers – needing to win to try to prove that they are better than others; losing only cements their view that they are useless.

- Bullying others – making other children feel bad can subconsciously make them feel better.

When a child displays their uncomfortable feelings via their actions, externalising their anxieties, not only is the resulting behaviour difficult to cope with, it is also upsetting – because all parents want their children to be confident and have good self-esteem. Some parents may even be concerned that their child has too high self-esteem or confidence, believing this to be the reason for their child's narcissistic, antisocial and unempathic behaviour. In this instance, however, they are mistaken. A child with high self-esteem and confidence is one who is emotionally stable; they have no need to try to belittle others or gain control over situations. Children who appear to be arrogant and too sure of themselves, on the other hand, are actually struggling with low levels of self-esteem and confidence, but putting on an act of bravado to try to fool others. Their insecurity underpins their antisocial behaviour, even though it would appear that they have no problem with self-doubt.

Once again, as you go through this chapter, remember the 'Why? How? What?' framework: why is your child struggling with self-esteem? How are they feeling? And what do you want to achieve in terms of changing their thoughts and beliefs through gentle-discipline methods?

What causes low self-esteem or a lack of confidence in children?

There are some wonderful ways to boost your child's self-esteem and confidence, which will help both them and you – them, because they will feel so much happier about themselves; and you, because a happy child is far less likely to behave in undesirable ways. Let's look at some of them now.

A fixed mindset

If children believe that they can't do something, they create a self-fulfilling prophecy: the more they think that they can't do it, the more likely it is that they will be unable to. Ability is not fixed at birth – it can always be changed – but the biggest hurdle is belief. Children with a fixed mindset may say things like, 'I can't do it, it's not even worth me trying; you do it', or, 'I'm so useless at maths, I'll never be good at it', or, 'I can't swim, I don't want to try.'

When children have a fixed mindset, they accept their often imaginary flaws and don't try to change them. As this mindset grows, it dents their self-esteem and confidence more and more. Ultimately, they can reach a point of believing that they are useless, but that there is nothing that they can do to change this.

Bullying

If a child is bullied by their peers, or even their parents and siblings, particularly verbally, their self-esteem and confidence quickly erode. They often start to believe what their aggressors are saying about them and think that they are useless and that's why they are being picked on. The sad part here is that bullies often target children who are unconfident or who struggle with their self-esteem, which only heightens the problem. And bullies themselves can struggle with self-esteem, which is why they try to make others feel bad. This is a cycle that can continue in a never-ending fashion, as children who are bullied are more likely to bully others.

Praise

We have already looked at praise in some depth (see pages 82–5), but it's important that we revisit it. Many believe that if their children have low self-esteem and a lack of confidence, the answer is to heap on the praise, telling them how wonderful they are almost constantly. Sadly, however, this often has the opposite effect. Why? Because they then feel that their parents' love for them is based upon their achievements – the less they achieve, the less they feel loved. Also, if the praise stops, it can cause a sharp nose-dive in self-belief and, if they are praised for things that are fixed, such as their looks, they find that there is little or nothing that they can do to change these attributes when they realise that the praise isn't wholly true.

Extrinsic motivation

Having previously looked at the issue of extrinsic versus intrinsic motivation (see page 75), we understand that the more a child is externally motivated to do something, the less chance there is that they will want to do something of their own accord. Children who are constantly rewarded for doing things can often develop a gross lack of motivation and a lack of self-esteem. This is because their self-esteem hinges solely on whatever rewards they do or don't get, and they never get to experience the thrill of doing something just because it feels good or because it makes them feel proud of themselves.

Labelling

Statements like 'Don't be silly', 'You're so clumsy' or 'You drive me mad' have little impact on children in the present, but over time they begin to erode their confidence and belief in themselves. In essence, they start to believe what you say about them. And once they believe the negative comments they hear about themselves they start to embody what is said about them, which serves only to dent their confidence more. So what you say now really does matter. The same is true for shaming children on purpose to try to change how they behave. This will never improve the way they act, but it could seriously affect their self-esteem and confidence, which is likely to make their behaviour regress even more.

Helicopter parenting

Rushing to keep children out of danger, fix problems before they even exist and monitor everything that they do at all times is a huge risk to confidence and self-esteem. Ultimately, each time that you hover or charge in to protect your child when they don't really need it, what you are saying to your child is: 'I don't trust you to be able to do this alone.' This makes your child feel that they are incapable of being independent. Unsurprisingly, growing up in a helicopter household often produces unconfident children with self-esteem difficulties.

Ignoring difficult emotions

We have already discussed in some detail the problems with ignoring bad behaviour, punishing tantrums by putting children in time out and not responding when children whine or swear. Each time we respond, or rather don't respond, in this manner we say to our child: 'I can't cope with your feelings, or with you.' The child begins to feel that their emotions are invalid, or don't matter, which, in turn, leads them to doubt their own self-worth. Even when we are not ignoring them, we can still increase the likelihood that they will feel this way by saying things like, 'Don't be silly, you're OK', 'Stop crying now', or, 'Calm down, stop being so angry.' We may say these things with good intentions, but the message that our children receive is that they are not good enough unless they are always calm. And, if they cannot calm themselves down (and we know they can't from a brain-development point of view), they are left feeling that they are inferior.

How to increase self-esteem and confidence

Helping a child to feel good about themselves is one of the most enjoyable and fulfilling parts of gentle discipline. Let's look at some of the ways in which you can help. (This list is by no means exhaustive – I recommend that you come up with ways that are unique to your family and child as well.)

Unconditional love

Helping a child to feel loved unconditionally, regardless of their behaviour or abilities, must always come first. You cannot increase a child's self-esteem or confidence without starting from this point. Only when they feel loved by their parents for who they are can they begin to love themselves. Going back to Maslow's hierarchy of needs (see page 40), we know that children must feel a sense of belonging and love in order to develop self-esteem and feel good about themselves. The key is in not trying to change your child, but accepting them as they are – the good and the bad. Listen intently to everything that they have to say and always be there for them. Help them to calm down when they are sad or angry and don't ignore their behaviour or the feelings behind it, no matter how tempted you are to do so. Lastly, don't punish or shame them and don't use exclusion from you – whether that's being shut in their rooms, in time out or on the naughty step – as a way to handle undesirable behaviour. When you do this, the message that you give to them is that you only want to be around them when they are 'good'. In other words, there is a part of their personality that you really don't like. The result? They begin to dislike themselves.

Develop their problem–solving skills

Every time you swoop in and fix something for your child, whether resolving a sibling argument, completing a jigsaw puzzle or helping with homework, you deprive your child of the ability to sort it out themselves. Giving your child some space to solve their own problems does wonders for increasing their self-esteem and confidence. If they think they can't do something, help them to know that you trust that they can – 'That looks really tricky; I have faith in you though' – and to think critically and logically, knowing this is something they struggle to do alone. Asking questions is a great way to trigger their problem-solving ability: 'Do you think that the shape you need has a straight side or a bobbly side?' Or, 'Can you think of anything that would help here?' Each problem that your child solves, as independently as possible, will help to build their self-esteem and confidence.

Tell them how you feel about them

Most of us are forthcoming with insults and criticism of our children or non-specific praise, but how often do we really tell them how we feel about them? Taking time to look properly at a picture that they have painted and commenting on how you like the colours they have chosen, telling them how proud they make you feel and saying that you've noticed how hard they have been trying to master a handstand, for example, can all really help your child to feel loved and seen.

As children get older it can be a little harder to do this, especially if they reply, 'Oh Mum, you're so embarrassing. Stop it.' At first, it may seem that they don't want you to tell them how you feel about them any more, but that Rubicon crossing (see page 172) just means you have to do it in a different way – because we all like to know when others think well of us, however old we are. My favourite approach in the tween and teen years is to write notes to each other. I have also been known to email or text them too. After a tricky period with my (then) eleven-year-old son we had a really lovely day together, and afterwards I wrote a note and pinned it onto his noticeboard in an envelope with his name on. It said something like this:

I just wanted to write you a note to tell you how much I loved today – it's been such a lovely day, thank you so much. You were really helpful and it makes me so proud to see how much you like to help other people.
See you tomorrow. I love you very much.
Mum xxx

The next morning I found a note on my pillow. He had written back to me:

Dear Mum,
I really liked your note, thank you for writing it. It really made me smile. I'm pleased that you appreciated me helping you, I really enjoyed it too.

Occasionally, I have been known to write notes and pop them into their lunch boxes or school bags, particularly if they are feeling worried about something. My nine-year-old daughter and I also have a wonderful book, which prompts us to write notes to each other. There are pages with questions, so that we can find out more about each other, but also spaces where she can write her concerns and worries. I've noticed that when she is feeling happy and secure the book is rarely used, but that it comes out again when she is feeling anxious or sad. (I've included details of the book in the Further Reading and Support and Resources section on page 266. Unfortunately, there isn't a version of the book for boys, which is a real shame and shows how gender-stereotyped our society is when it comes to expressing emotions and the mistaken belief that boys don't – or don't want to – do it.)

Opportunities for independence

In the same way that you should encourage children to solve their own problems, you also need to let them take care of their own needs as much as possible. If a task is age-appropriate, allow them to complete it unaided, to make them feel capable and confident. Too many parents take on tasks for their children that they are capable of doing themselves. And each time that they do so, they take away some of the confidence and self-esteem that accompany the sense of achievement and feelings of 'I did it!'

Giving children special responsibilities around the house or at school can help too. If your child struggles at school, asking their teachers to consider giving them a job, such as delivering the register or collecting the post, can make a big difference.

Also, make sure that you do not force your own unfilled wishes and regrets onto your child. Allow them to choose their own activities and hobbies and their own life path as much as possible. If you wanted to take ballet classes when you were young, but for some reason didn't, don't force it on your child. They need to make their own choices and decisions, free from your influence, as often as they can.

Encourage a growth mindset

Help your child to know that it is OK for them to doubt themselves, it is OK to be nervous and it is OK to make mistakes – everybody does. Then, help them to recognise these feelings when they have them and perhaps give them a special name – even a human one. Ask them to be aware of the feelings when they arise and tell them to 'go away'. Next, give them a positive replacement – tell them to reframe each negative feeling and to keep repeating the positive replacement, either silently or out loud, depending on the location.

Here are some examples of negative, 'fixed', statements and their positive, or 'growth', replacements:

Negative, Fixed, Belief Statements	Positive, Growth, Belief Statements
I can't tie my shoelaces, I'm useless.	Tying my shoelaces is tricky, but I'm learning how to do it.
I'm really bad at sports at school.	Right now, I don't do well in sports, but I know if I practise hard, I will get much better.
Nobody wants to be friends with me.	I struggle with making friends at the moment, but I'm working on being more confident and introducing myself to others and asking them to play.
I can't do my maths homework.	I'm really struggling with my maths homework, but I'm not going to give up. I know if I really concentrate and ask for help, I can do it.
I can't climb the tree; I'm rubbish.	Climbing isn't something I'm good at right now, but I bet the other children weren't good to start with. I can get better at it, just as they did.

Affirmations

Affirmations may sound a bit 'new age', but they can be incredibly powerful. They are simply positive statements that your child either speaks out loud and repeats several times daily (or they can listen to pre-recorded ones on a download or CD – see page 268 for a recommended supplier).

Here are some examples of affirmations:

- Each day, in every way, I am becoming more confident.

- I accept myself just as I am; I am more than enough.

- I can do anything I want to do so long as I believe that I can.

- I am me; it is good to be me.

- I trust that I can achieve whatever I want.

- My confidence is growing every day.

Encourage your child to write their own affirmations – the more personal they are, the more likely they are to believe them. Next, encourage them to say them every day, looking in the mirror, if they feel comfortable doing so. You could also record them, so that they can play them as they go to sleep each night.

Real family case studies

Let's finish the chapter once more on some real family situations, this time concerning children struggling with self-esteem and confidence. As you read through them, see if you can pick out the symptoms of their struggles and what may have caused them – the 'Why?' and the 'How?' – and think about the 'What?' too: what would you hope to achieve in terms of discipline?

Q: *My nine-year-old son is the eldest of my three boys and is a quiet, shy, sensitive boy who is very bright. He has always felt more comfortable with rules and knowing his boundaries. He has always liked quite repetitive behaviour: when he was younger he liked to sit on the same spot on the mat and in classes at school. He is what many would describe as a 'good boy'. I know it's not a great term but he just is; he likes to be 'good' and do what is asked of him, and he struggles to just relax about that. I almost have to push him to 'break the rules' a bit!*

Anyway, the issue we have, and have always had since he was tiny, is how he reacts to losing. He will start with outright lying and changing the rules or score to try to make it that he wins. If the other person (especially his younger brother) playing doesn't go along with that, it will build to complete meltdown, tears, sometimes fighting (the only fight he has had at school was because of this). More often than not we have to stop the game, as he will not accept that he has lost. Or even if he just starts to lose he starts to cheat and lie. He is OK if he is playing a group game, like football (he is on a team) – he'll get a bit fed up, but abides by the rules, etc.

He is incredibly stubborn and hard to negotiate with. He will stand his ground and will not back down (which is why we normally end up abandoning the game). I have tried everything over the years and had hoped it would get better as he got older, but that hasn't happened yet.

A: I think your son is really struggling with his self-esteem and confidence levels. His need to always win competitive games when he is playing solo is characteristic of this and the lying and lack of acceptance of losing cements this idea. Children who have issues with their self-esteem and confidence will often lie about winning to make themselves feel better. Fighting about it is common too, the premise being that if they can make somebody else feel bad, they may make themselves feel better. Cognitive dissonance plays a role too. If the child lies, they avoid having to admit to themselves that they are 'a loser'. The stubborn behaviour and refusal to listen when you try to explain to him is also a form of this.

You say that your son is quite shy. This also reflects a

lack of self-confidence. I suspect the fact that he has two other brothers doesn't help matters, especially if they are better than him at certain things, or if you praise them for things that he doesn't get praised for. Praise in itself is actually a problem, as is rewarding for achievement. Both of these increase extrinsic motivation, but undermine intrinsic motivation and self-esteem.

I would suggest that you remove any games in your house that are not 'co-operative' and instead focus on your son's feelings and increasing his well-being. The most important thing is that he feels he is loved unconditionally – not just when he is a 'good boy', but when he is acting out too. In fact, this is when he needs you more. If he loses at something, sit with him, offer him a hug and say, 'It's tough losing, isn't it, especially when we really want to win? You know that it's not a reflection of how clever you are don't you?' I would also really work on making him feel good about himself. Sharing stories specifically written to increase self-esteem and listening to CDs that feature affirmations can help him move from a fixed mindset of insecurity and doubt to one where he understands that his abilities are in his hands and he can shape his life however he wishes. Try to spend lots of time with him away from his brothers and tell him how much you enjoy his company. You could also try writing notes and slipping them into his lunch box now and again, just reminding him how much you love him and how proud you are of him. Take care to not label him, shame him or talk negatively about his behaviour in front of him or compare him to his siblings. It's important that whatever he overhears about himself is positive.

It sounds like he's quite low at the moment, so you can expect several more outbursts over the next few months while you are implementing all of this, but hopefully it should produce some good results in time.

Q: *My six-year-old son hits himself and shouts that he is rubbish if he has done something wrong, even if we don't tell him off (which we generally don't, as we try to be as gentle as possible). He seems to feel negative emotions in a big way, whining or screaming wordlessly if he is asked to do something he doesn't want to do or if he is gently corrected when he has made a mistake. How do we go about showing him when he has made a mistake and teaching him the right way when he reacts so badly to such situations? It has been brought to our attention that he does this at school also, but it seems they are implying he is disruptive, when we can clearly see the extreme behaviour is a result of negative emotions.*

A: I'm sorry to hear that your son is struggling so much. My suggestion is that almost all of his behaviour is related to a lack of self-esteem and confidence. The fact that he calls himself 'rubbish' highlights that he is really having problems with his self-belief. The hitting is a form of externalising his dislike of himself. Some children hit out at and bully others when they are feeling bad about themselves; your son has chosen to take this behaviour out upon himself, which in some ways is better, as he's not hurting others, but also more alarming because he is self-harming.

It is imperative that you help your son to feel loved unconditionally. Never punish or shame him; never, importantly, ignore his behaviour, no matter how negative it is; and never, ever put him in time out or similar. Your son needs lots of attention and help when he feels bad – the worse his behaviour, the more he needs your support. There is nothing wrong with big feelings, but it is hard to handle them when you only have six years of brain development.

Next time your son's emotions explode, say to him, 'I'm here for you, can I help?' Sit as close to him as he will allow and wait until he is ready. Offer him a big cuddle and say: 'You seem really mad about something. Can you tell me about it so I can help?' Ideally, his teacher should do similar at school. Every time his behaviour is silenced through ignoring, distraction or punishment they, and you, are subconsciously telling him that you don't like him, even if that's not what you mean. This then makes him feel even more alone and worse about himself, and his behaviour will rapidly go into a downward spiral. Even if the tantrums stopped and he was quiet, ignoring or punishment will still generate the feelings, but they will be aimed inwards even more. You must allow him a safe space and the security to let them out.

Once you have allowed the emotions to flow, you need to focus on rebuilding him. Help him to have better beliefs about himself: he is not rubbish, he just hasn't had enough practice to master something yet. Let him know that with effort and focus he can achieve anything he wants, and his efforts make you so very proud of him. Spend lots of time telling him how much you love him and helping him with things he struggles with, but try not to take over. Instead, help him to develop problem-solving skills, so that he can achieve things alone. Lastly, I would think about putting him in charge of something special at home – perhaps arranging the fruit in the fruit bowl each week when you unpack your shopping. Tell him how important that job is and how you know you can trust him with it. Comment on the display of fruit and on the effort he put into the job and tell him how much you appreciate his work.

This is not a short-term fix. You will need to give him unconditional love and support and help build his confidence and esteem for a long while to come, but it's great that you've noticed the problem while he's so young, as that gives you plenty of time to work on this.

As I mentioned in my response to the parent above, there is no short-term fix for boosting confidence and self-esteem. Regardless of how old your child is, support and unconditional love remain two of the most important gifts you can give them. The more loved – no matter what – and supported a child feels, the more likely they are to behave in ways that make everybody happy.

Chapter 14

Working with Parental Demons

You now know why children act the way that they do and the best ways to cope with their behaviour, but next comes the biggest challenge of all: working on yourself. Knowledge is one thing, action is another, and if there is one major hurdle to overcome when putting gentle discipline into action it is you, the parent. Most of what we've examined in this book applies as much to you as to your child: how confident do you feel? Do you have belief in yourself? Are your beliefs fixed or not? And perhaps most importantly of all, how do you manage your own emotions – particularly anger? Let's look at a few of the parental demons that can get in the way of successful gentle discipline.

Aiming for good enough

All parents make mistakes. We all have days that we are not proud of. We all make sacrifices and compromises. None of us is perfect, but it is our mistakes that are most important in terms of our growth as parents. Each time we don't quite do our best, we can learn and we can teach our children how to handle disappointment, failure and getting it wrong. We can teach them grace, honesty and humility.

When I run parenting workshops, I always speak about the 70/30 rule: trying to be the best parent you can be 70 per cent of the time and not worrying too much about the other 30 per cent. If you can get through an average day feeling good about your parenting about 70 per cent of the time, then it's OK if there's 30 per cent you're not so proud of. I like to think of this as a daily quota that resets at midnight each night.

I am not perfect. In part, I do what I do because I've been where you are and made as many mistakes as you have, but want you to know you can still make it through the other side with your goals to parent gently intact. The thing is, parenting is hard work. It's harder than anything else I've ever done. And, as children get older, it doesn't get easier – it just changes. We have to try to balance this with work, adult relationships and keeping a roof over our heads and food on the table. It is not possible to be everything to everyone. A much more realistic goal to aim for is to be 'good enough'. And I feel that 70 per cent *is* good enough. That doesn't mean not trying for the remaining 30 per cent of the time, however. The key with gentle discipline is always trying to be mindful and respectful, even though there will be times when you know the 'right' thing to do, but for various reasons it simply isn't possible or doesn't work quickly enough. In those times, I truly believe that doing your best, whatever your best is, is fine – as long as it's 30 per cent of the time or less and that you forgive yourself when it happens. So when you don't parent in quite the way you desire, move on; don't throw in the towel and think, I screwed up, I might as well give up this gentle-discipline lark. Your best – the times when you get it 'right' – is good enough:

the times where you counted to ten and responded with compassion and understanding; the times when you connected
when you least felt like it. They are the times that matter. And,
if they are in the majority, that's good enough – good enough
to raise the type of individual you hope for: one who tries their
best, but understands and accepts the times, and themselves,
when they cannot.

In fact, the 30-per-cent times can often be more valuable
than the rest. These are the times that are eye-opening: they
show us what we need to work on within ourselves – our trigger points, how to cope with our temper and anger, the areas
we need to concentrate more on with our children, and how
to turn a bad situation into something positive that we can
use as a learning experience for our children and apologise to
them. They also show us where and when we are not looking
after ourselves, and our own needs, enough. If your 30 per cent
starts to creep up, it is a sure sign that you need support and
a breathing space. This might mean you need physical space,
or you might need physical help; you might need somebody
to talk to or, sometimes, you need to simply forgive yourself.
Whatever your need, it takes priority. Nobody can nurture
anybody or anything else effectively if they need to nurture
themselves.

So starting tomorrow, keep a tally of your percentages in
mind. The chances are that on most days your ratio will look
something like 90/10, but there will also be 50/50 days and
even the odd 40/60 day. On these days, rather than attacking
your own self-worth and self-esteem, see it as a sign that you
need to give yourself a break: celebrate the 70, 80 and 90 days –
let them build your confidence and belief in yourself. You are
good enough.

Coping with unwanted opinions and advice

Have you ever been given parenting advice that goes against your beliefs? I certainly have! Much of the advice we hear from others about our children and our parenting is well meant. However, when you are on the receiving end, it can be hard to see any positivity in these comments:

> You should just ignore his tantrums; that will teach him that nobody's watching, so he'll stop.

> If she spoke to me like that, I would lock her in her room for the rest of the day.

> You need to be firmer with them. A quick tap on the hand worked in my day when children behaved badly.

> Ignore it when he does something naughty and heap the praise on him when he's good; that way, he'll get a reward for being good, but not for being naughty.

Criticism of any sort is hard to stomach, but that which relates to the way we raise our children is surely the hardest to receive. This is because not only are you and your abilities being attacked, but the behaviour and personality of your child is too. And this hurts. Understanding the motivation behind the criticism is almost always the best way to handle it. So let's look at this in more detail.

First, the advice is well meant – because people care about you. It can be really hard to see friends or family suffer. How would you feel if your sister always looked tired and drawn?

You would be worried, wouldn't you? And if you felt you could clearly pinpoint the reason behind this, and a possible solution, wouldn't you be tempted to discuss it with them? This is the position many friends and family members are in when they criticise their nearest and dearest. Their advice may be anything but helpful to you, and you may feel that you are being undermined, but the motivation behind what they are saying is entirely altruistic. They care about you and they can't bear to see you suffer. In this instance, you need to help your friends and family to understand your choices and see why their solutions aren't for you. Make sure you let them know how much you value their concern though and thank them for their thoughtfulness.

The second reason for unwanted advice and criticism is because others don't understand your choices, particularly the older generation. Your grandmother may not appreciate why you repeatedly allow your son to tantrum; in her day, children would have been given a swift smack on the behind, which would have fixed their behaviour, for their own good, so that they would grow to be polite and respectful adults. She may be fearful that if you don't 'toughen up', your son will be anything but. The best response here is to carefully explain your reasoning, using articles, books and the like to support your position, especially if they are publications to which the person in question can relate.

The third reason for criticism is because you are doing things differently from the way you were raised. This is likely to come from your parents in particular. You may have been smacked or sent to your room for the same behaviour that prompts you to give your son a hug and ask how he is feeling. Your mother might suggest that you do what she did to you, saying that you've turned out fine. The fact that you've chosen a different path can be perceived by her as a criticism of the way that you were brought up. When you respond, try to understand that it can be hard for parents to learn that the way they raised their children has since been proven to be suboptimal or even dangerous. Try to explain your choices using sensitive and carefully chosen words, letting them know how scientific understanding has moved on. Tell them that your choices are not meant to reflect disapproval of how they parented. Parenting is full of very personal decisions and these are yours.

The last underlying reason for criticism is the rarest, but it can be by far the hardest to handle. The people in this category who give advice and criticism are usually ones who, somewhere along the line, were hurt deeply and covered that hurt with bitterness. It is easier for them to attack others than to deal with their own failures and shortcomings. Sadly, these people rarely, if ever, change. In terms of a response here, in most cases it is simply better to accept that the criticism is not about you or your family. It says far more about the person doing the criticising than it does about you. The best thing you can do is to smile and ignore the comment, or simply say, 'Thank you for your advice, I will consider it', and move on. Worst-case scenario, it might be sensible to cut ties, if possible – or, if not, to keep meetings with the person in question to a minimum.

Questioning your approach to discipline

Sometimes, receiving criticism from others, particularly those close to us, can cause us to question our parenting. If results are slow to appear, or we find ourselves unable to cope or figure out what to do, we can be at our most vulnerable. While writing this book, I asked some parents what they did if something, or somebody, caused them to doubt their gentle-discipline approach.

Here are some of their answers:

I put myself in my daughter's shoes and ask myself how I would want and expect to be treated. I always come back to the same conclusion: you can never be too kind or respectful.

I go to parenting groups on social media and ask for reassurance or advice.

I find that I have to take a step back, think of all the good things we've achieved so far and try and reconnect with my gut instinct that supports this way of parenting. With regards to advice from others, I try not to rise to it, thank them for their kind thoughts and input (after all, they are only trying to help), but politely decline or ignore it. I find that by talking everything through with my husband we reaffirm the way we want to do things and why.

I go back to my core philosophies and think, Would XYZ help? Plus, is my boy healthy and happy? How is he developing on the whole, rather than how has the last week gone?

I ask myself, would I prefer if my child was more like X [whoever is giving advice's] child? The answer is usually no, which means I'm happy doing what I'm doing.

I remind myself of the successes we have had through parenting gently, spend time with those who are like-minded, whether virtually or in reality, and remember the evidence for this being the way we want to parent.

I remind myself why we parent the way we do and what our long-term goals are for our daughter. And I just don't care about what others think, as their parenting style is different and I don't want to parent their way. I want to parent our way with our daughter the way that works for us.

Sometimes, when things get difficult, I wonder whether I'm getting it all wrong. Then I look at my children, I watch them experiencing a deep emotion and try to feel what they feel. It's only once I allow it reach my heart that I accept that even if things aren't going smoothly, in the end I'm learning from them much more than teaching them.

I think it's just about belief – a feeling, an instinct that I'm doing the right thing, not overthinking it, just going by what feels right and trusting that. That doesn't mean that there isn't doubt sometimes. It's hard with all the noise of parenting advice, but I feel able to separate myself from all of that and just do what feels like it makes sense for my little girl. I really do believe I'm doing the right thing by her.

I think of the people I want my children to be when they are older and how I want them to remember their childhood. I tell myself that I am trying to be the best parent that I can.

I attempt to think long-term and remind myself that quick fixes to stop certain behaviours do not deal with the root of the issue. I think of how my brother and I were disciplined as children (plenty of punishments, smacks and insults) and remember how awful it felt and the lasting negative effects it had on our relationships with our parents and our own confidence. I do not want to repeat that with my kid.

When I'm questioning my parenting methods, I also try to take a step back and assess if the problem is me or my child. Most often, it's me and it helps to take some time to think about what I want, what my child wants and how we can come to an agreement. And I try to be honest with myself, and answer the question, 'Is this really important or are you just digging your heels in?'

How to get your partner on board with gentle discipline

Ideally, parenting style is something that all adults will discuss with their partner before they have children. As well as researching birth plans and nursery products, I truly believe that discussing parenting opinions is vital before the first baby arrives. Too many couples only realise that they have opposing views on parenting several months or years down the line. So as well as writing a birth plan, parents-to-be should also write a parenting plan, thinking about common scenarios and how they might respond to them. I particularly love it when a pregnant couple attend one of my gentle-discipline talks or workshops.

But what do you do if the differences in your parenting beliefs only surface further down the line? First, you have to acknowledge your partner's feelings and try to understand where they come from. Often, if somebody has been raised in a certain way (and say, 'It never did me any harm'), for the other partner to say that they would like to do things differently is a bit of an insult to their in-laws. Acknowledging this is an important first step. Next, ask your partner (without judgement) why they feel the way they do and how they would deal with certain scenarios. Also, ask if they know of any research to back up their thoughts.

Once you have thoroughly listened to your partner, explain to them how you feel, why you feel the way you do and offer a brief synopsis of any supporting research. Consider media they may like. Do they read blogs, magazine articles or books or do they prefer videos or podcasts? Perhaps they would do better with 'in-person' learning, such as workshops. Be careful of the wording you use here. Don't use accusatory language: 'You're really rough when you shout', or, 'When you did that it really scared her.' Instead, use 'I' statements and clarify your emotions – 'I feel uncomfortable when you shout at her', for example.

The next step is to try to agree on tiny baby steps, rather than everything at once. Perhaps your partner will agree to change their language slightly and drop the word 'naughty' or similar for a week or two. That's enough to start with. Don't try for too much too soon. The next decision could be to try to stop threatening punishments and instead use empathising language. The beauty of gentle discipline is that results are fairly obvious. They may be slow (sometimes, frustratingly so), but there will be a 'breakthrough' moment that makes your partner think, Wow, that worked. Deal with one issue at a time and maintain open (and non-accusatory/non-judgemental) discussion throughout.

It can also be really helpful to meet up with others disciplining the same way as you, particularly those of the same gender as your partner. Role modelling is very powerful and often many of us lack this when it comes to parenting.

Dealing with your own anger

I am convinced that many people who say they never lose their temper with their children are either lying, delusional or simply haven't been a parent for very long. All parents 'lose it' at some point with their children, including me.

Personally, I have found it harder to keep my cool the older my children get. My first real 'red-mist' moment didn't happen until towards the end of the toddler years. Since then, they have been more regular than I would care to admit. That's life. Nobody is perfect. As I've said, there is nothing wrong with anger – it's a normal human emotion and is actually a very useful one sometimes. The problem is the way we deal with it, especially in front of our children.

Why parents get angry

I think it's important to start by saying that something can trigger even the most placid person at some point in their life. In many cases though, anger, particularly the type that makes us act in ways we never normally would, can be averted if we understand our triggers. The following all play a role in our levels of anger – some can be avoided and others can be worked on, whether by ourselves or with the help of a professional:

- Growing up in a home where verbal or physical violence was the norm

- Physical exhaustion (including improper nourishment and deficiencies)

- Mental exhaustion

- Lack of support from family, especially partners

- Financial worries

- Stress from looking after elderly or sick relatives

- Work worries

- A lack of time to ourselves, particularly time to unwind and 'breathe'

- Friendship or relationship problems

In my own case, anger is my default setting because of my own upbringing. My parents were wonderful and I loved them very dearly, but my mum was a 'shouter'. Understandably, I grew up to be a shouter too and I have to really work to stop that being my initial response to any issues with my own children. My other big triggers for anger are work stress (either from working too much or absorbing too many emotions from my clients) and a lack of looking after myself properly in terms of nourishment and relaxation time.

As with all things, prevention is better than cure where anger is concerned. I know now, after many years of observing my own feelings and parenting, when I need to take 'time out'. I can recognise my early-warning signs; I know when I've neglected self-care and I can usually schedule in an emergency top-up before I lose my cool. I budget money each month for looking after myself, which I use to pay for a weekly Pilates class and a monthly massage and reflexology session. This level of self-care may be out of some people's reach financially, but I see it as a household expense – it keeps me running well and I can take care of our home and the kids as a result. Yes, it means I forfeit new clothes and don't have much of a social life, but I cannot parent without it. If you cannot find any spare money for self-care, then invest time instead: a long walk, a candlelit bath, a phone call with an old friend, some time spent meditating …

Coping 'in the moment'

Practising mindfulness is my saving grace. I don't mean mindfulness in terms of listening to relaxation CDs every day, although that certainly is great. I mean living 'in the moment' – being aware of what is happening inside me and really observing my feelings. This helps me to pause before responding. Often, anger, as a response to our children's actions, is unjust or unwarranted – certainly in the degree to which we release it. My friend PETER helps me out when I'm really struggling in these scenarios:

- **P** = Pause: don't react immediately.

- **E** = Empathise: try to understand how your child is, or was, feeling and their point of view.

- **T** = Think: think about different ways you could respond and the learning that would happen as a result.

- **E** = Exhale: take a deep breath, breathe out, relax your shoulders and picture your anger leaving your body.

- **R** = Respond: now is the time to respond to your child, not before.

There are many other coping tips too. The list is infinite, but these are some of my favourites:

- Wear five red bands on your right wrist. Each time you override your anger when responding to your child, move a band to your left hand. Your goal is for all five bands to be on the left by the end of the day.

- Close your eyes and picture yourself in your favourite place: a beach, a forest, a mountain. Take yourself off there for a minute or two when you're most in need of peace.

- Picture somebody who always seems calm and cool. Imagine stepping inside their body and wearing it as a suit. Feel how calm they are and let the peace soak into your own body. Think about how they might respond to situations that trigger your anger.

- Call a friend or have a good rant on an internet discussion group – one used by people with a similar mindset to yours.

- Take a parental 'time out'. If all else fails, make sure your child is safe in a childproofed space and take yourself off to another room to calm down for a couple of minutes.

What should you do if you lose your cool?

There will be times when you cannot control your temper. When this happens accept it, forgive yourself and move on. Everybody has bad days. Don't give up, you're not a bad parent. Giving up on gentle discipline because of a bad day is like getting your new shoes dirty in a muddy puddle and then rolling in it and covering yourself in mud because you 'failed'. You didn't. You can wash the shoes off and keep them clean tomorrow. But learn from what happened; don't let it go to waste. Identify your triggers and what you could have done differently at each point. And, perhaps most importantly, take time to calm down and then apologise to your child. Children are more resilient than we think. If they are older, this is a good time to discuss with them that feeling angry is OK, but being violent in voice or body is not. Tell them that you made a mistake, that you will try to do better next time. If you're feeling run down and short of patience, ask your children to help you. Tell them you feel highly strung today and would really appreciate their help to keep things calm. You'll be surprised at their response!

Real parents' strategies for coping with anger

I asked some parents for their suggestions for dealing with anger in response to their children's behaviour. As you can see, each response is beautifully unique, which is why I am not giving you a set of instructions to follow. You need to find what works for you – because something definitely will, just as it does for these parents:

When I'm close to losing my temper, I give myself a time out: I walk away, go into the kitchen or the garden and take a deep breath.

I try to break the mood by doing something to make us laugh, usually tickling or putting music on and doing silly dancing. Hearing their laughter makes me feel better instantly.

When my child triggers uncomfortable feelings in me I take a good look at them. I have grown so much in myself from addressing these feelings. It is not my child's job to help me grow, but I have to go through some uncomfortable stuff to become the parent I want to be. Parenting is a very humbling experience.

I say, 'I love you' (as if to remind myself!) when things are getting stressful. It helps me to be 'present' and not just reacting and focusing on my own needs at that moment.

I try to step back for a second and tell myself that there is a reason for his behaviour – he's overtired or overstimulated or bored or wants some attention – and do my best to deal with it accordingly. Telling myself that he is not giving me a hard time, he is *having* a hard time, sometimes helps.

Of course, every now and then the moment gets away from you, and you might snap. But it's OK to admit when you're wrong – let your child know that your emotions got too big to handle and apologise. You can't do everything right all the time. I think it is important that your child sees you as just as fallible as they are, and learns how to deal with mistakes.

Ten per cent of the time I lose it and become Shouty Mummy. Ninety per cent of the time I stop, leave the room, gather my thoughts and try to find out what the issue is.

I try to leave and breathe (my daughter almost never lets me leave!). I try to ask why? Why am I reacting this way? Why is she acting this way?

If I'm feeling a bit exasperated, then we put our boots on and go outside to see the chickens!

I sometimes go in a room and shut the door if I'm frustrated. But I haven't done that in a long while. I've now managed to understand there's a reason for all unhappy behaviour, so the challenge is trying to guess the problem. It's like a personal challenge to find a quick solution to my son's problem.

If I'm getting cross too often, I make sure I get some time for me and some sleep.

I breathe deeply and remind myself who out of the pair of us doesn't yet have the skills to manage big emotions and then I centre myself and be his centre.

When my daughter whines and gets super-sensitive to the slightest change of tone from me, I kneel down, tell her I love her and give her a hug. She usually needs that hug. Then I listen carefully about the (to her) *so* important thing and I realise there is always a reason why she is reacting the way she is. Often, I also call my husband at work and whine to him and he always has something positive to say that reassures and calms me down. When he is home he can also take the child who is driving me up the wall to calm them, and I get a few minutes to sit in our room and calm down myself. I never knew 'go to your room' could be something I would love to hear.

What to do on days when you feel like giving up

As with most things in life, often the right decision is not the easiest. As you have probably realised by now, there are no quick fixes for behaviour problems, at least not ones that don't come at a great cost in the long term. Gentle discipline demands a lot of you as a parent. It is hard work and often relentless. On my down days I have a recurring thought: I don't want to be an adult any more. On these days, I fantasise about what it would feel like to be a child again and focus on how easy it was in comparison to being a parent.

Thankfully, these days are few and far between – definitely fewer as my children get older, as I mellow a little and become more confident in what I am doing. The same will apply to you too. In the meantime, don't just fantasise about that 'day off' – take it. Spend some time away from your children, for as long – and as far away – as you can manage emotionally, financially and practically. This will give you renewed energy and determination to continue on the gentle path. Taking time to look after yourself isn't a luxury, it is a necessity if you want to follow this parenting path. You cannot pour from an empty cup; you cannot gently discipline your child if you are not disciplined enough to take care of yourself. The moments when you feel like giving up are warnings that you need to look inwards, not outwards.

When I feel like throwing in the towel I ask myself why. Quite often the answer will be self-doubt or the fact that I'm scared that what I am doing is wrong. This fear is interesting; working on how to handle it is a game changer. You have two options, reminding us, once again, of fight-or-flight mode:

FEAR: Face Everything And Rise

or

FEAR: Forget Everything And Run

This time, however, the fight is internal, the only enemy being your own fixed mindset. Will you choose to face it and rise up, fuelled by the knowledge that you know you can do better, for both yourself and your child? Or will you choose to run away and give up on the idea of gentle discipline, despite everything you know about its benefits and the risks of mainstream discipline? I do hope that, after reading this book, you will be inspired to do the former.

Chapter 15

Your Journey to Gentle Discipline

To close, I would like to provide a little summary of what we have covered before you embark on your own journey. At the start of this book we considered the true meaning of discipline and how it differs significantly from what most believe it to be, namely punishment. Real – or gentle – discipline is all about teaching and learning, with the parent and child assuming either role. It is sad that there is a need to invent a new terminology – gentle discipline – to describe what should be just discipline, but so many people in society today are confused about its real meaning. The term gentle discipline helps in some way to differentiate it from the view most have.

One of the most common questions I am asked by parents of young children is: 'What age should you start to discipline?' The answer to that is by now (I hope) obvious: it is never too early to start. Discipline, after all, just means teaching and learning. So, from the very day your baby is born, you are already disciplining them. You, as a parent, are the greatest teacher your child will ever have; you are and will continue to be the biggest influence on their life and the development of their personality. That may sound like a forbidding task, but it gives you the most wonderful opportunity to foster the development of a kind, empathic, confident, independent, respectful and happy individual – and goodness knows, the world needs more of them. And the task is not as daunting as it sounds at first. You need do only three things: respect, understand and guide. Respect and understand your child's feelings and point of view, as well as their current capabilities, and gently guide them to do and be better. When you think of it like this, it is actually quite simple.

If you are reading this book as the parent of a teenager, it's never too late. You still have so many opportunities to change the way you are with them and to change the way that they are. Indeed, some of you reading this book might even take inspiration from it as ways to improve your adult relationships too.

When we looked at discipline as a form of teaching and learning, we examined why it is important to understand what you want to teach your child and how you will go about it. Discipline should always be mindful. Too many parents discipline because it is expected, and they are conscious of other people's opinions or of onlookers. But, as a teacher to your child, you are the only one who should decide when and how to discipline. Always remember this. The idea of being a good teacher is vital. You are the best and most influential role model your child will ever have. With this in mind, think about the qualities of a good teacher and try to embody them (see pages 7–8). Let's go back to the acronym SPACE, which helps us to be good teachers and discipline both fairly and effectively:

- Stay calm

- Proper expectations

- Affinity with your child

- Connect and contain emotions

- Explain and example

In order to have proper expectations, we must understand how a child's brain develops and, importantly, the most distinctive cognitive differences between adults and children, at least until they are teenagers or older. Young children struggle with empathy and Theory of Mind, or understanding that others feel differently to them. They also find critical, logical, abstract and hypothetical thought difficult, as well as, perhaps most significantly, impulse control. Adults have the ability and social filters to regulate their behaviour in a way that a child (of any age) cannot. And this is why so many mainstream discipline methods are ineffective – because they require a level of understanding and thought that is not usual in a young child. It is so important to remember this, and not simply punish the child for having a child's brain.

Next, while looking at the causes of many different undesirable behaviours commonly exhibited by children, we learned to ask ourselves three important questions: Why? How? What? Why is the child behaving this way? Has something triggered their behaviour? Is it developmentally normal? How is the child feeling? Are they acting this way because they are feeling bad? What do you hope to teach the child when you discipline them?

When it comes to the 'Why?', look for the underlying reason for the behaviour. If you don't, you are merely palliating and the cause remains, making the discipline ineffective. And the 'How?': most undesirable behaviour stems from an uncomfortable feeling in the child, for example sadness, anxiety, fear, anger, grief and more. You must attempt to understand how your child is feeling in order to be able to help them and appreciate how your discipline makes them feel. If you make them feel worse, the likelihood is that their behaviour will worsen too. And the 'What?' – if you do not know what the aim of your discipline is, then don't do anything. Your discipline is only effective when you have a goal in mind, because only then can you decide on the approach needed to fulfil it.

We considered the concept of being 'good enough'. No parent is perfect and we all make mistakes. Those mistakes are valuable too – they are how we learn to be better teachers. When you put into practice what you have learned in this book you will make mistakes, just as I do, and that's OK. Aiming for 70/30 is a more realistic goal than 100 per cent perfection.

Keeping a growth mindset and a belief that you can discipline your child both effectively and gently, even on your darkest parenting day, are also so important. You may struggle at the start, but every master was once a beginner – you just need to keep trying and stay consistent. I have faith that you can do it.

Lastly, we looked at parental demons and how our own behaviour can scupper even the best-laid discipline plans. We learned that it is vital to work on our own emotions, including coming to terms with our upbringing. And we also saw why taking care of our own needs is crucial too – it is a necessity, not a luxury, it is an essential piece of the gentle-discipline jigsaw. I also recommended taking the advice of my good friend Peter whenever you struggle with your feelings and need help responding to your child 'in the moment':

- **P** = Pause: don't react immediately.

- **E** = Empathise: try to understand how your child is, or was, feeling and their point of view.

- **T** = Think: think about different ways you could respond and the learning that would happen as a result.

- **E** = Exhale: take a deep breath, breathe out, relax your shoulders and picture your anger leaving your body.

- **R** = Respond: now is the time to respond to your child, not before.

Gentle discipline, in my opinion, is the most effective way to grow happy, confident, independent, polite, co-operative and successful children. Through both personal and professional experience, I have seen the amazing effects of a shift to a more compassionate and mindful approach. I have seen angry children become calm and withdrawn children become confident. I have seen sibling relationships flourish after a rocky start and fragile, disconnected relationships become strong and healthy. Gentle discipline may not be a quick fix, but it works, not just for a few weeks or months, but for ever. Indeed, it is life-changing, for both child and parent.

So are you ready to face everything and rise? You have all you need here to gently discipline your child successfully; now you just have to trust in yourself enough to believe that you can do it.

References

Chapter 1

1 McCann, D., Barrett, A., Cooper, A., Crumpler, D., Dalen, L., Grimshaw, K., Kitchen, E., Lok, K., Porteous, L., Prince, E., Sonuga-Barke, E., Warner, J. O. and Stevenson, J., 'Food additives and hyperactive behaviour in 3-year-old and 8/9-year-old children in the community: a randomised, double-blinded, placebo controlled trial', *Lancet*, 370 (2007), pp. 1560–67.

2 Montgomery, P., Burton, J., Sewell, R., Spreckelsen, T. and Richardson, A., 'Low blood long chain omega-3 fatty acids in UK children are associated with poor cognitive performance and behavior: a cross-sectional analysis from the DOLAB study', *PLoS One*, 8(6) (24 June 2013).

3 Lebourgeois, M., Wright, K., Lebourgeois, H. and Jenni, O., 'Dissonance Between Parent-Selected Bedtimes and Young Children's Circadian Physiology Influences Nighttime Settling Difficulties', *Mind Brain Education*, 7(4) (December 2013), pp. 234–42.

4 Carskadon, M., Wolfson, A., Acebo, C., Tzischinsky, O. and Seifer, R., 'Adolescent sleep patterns, circadian timing, and sleepiness at a transition to early school days', *Sleep*, 15;21(8) (December 1998), pp. 871–81.

5 Wright, H. and Lack, L., 'Effect of light wavelength on suppression and phase delay of the melatonin rhythm', *Chronobiology International*, 18(5) (September 2001), pp. 801–8.

6 Ben-Sasson, A., Carter, A. and Briggs-Gowan, M., 'Sensory Over-Responsivity in Elementary School: Prevalence and Social-Emotional Correlates', *Journal of Abnormal Child Psychology*, 37 (2009), pp. 705–16.

7 Ahn, R. R., Miller, L. J., Milberger, S. and McIntosh, D. N., 'Prevalence of parents' perceptions of sensory processing disorders among kindergarten children', *American Journal of Occupational Therapy*, 58 (2004), pp. 287–93.

8 Forest, M., Cathiard, A. and Bertrand, J., 'Evidence of Testicular Activity in Early Infancy', *Journal of Clinical Endocrinology and Metabolism*, 37(1) (2009).

9 Ostatníková, D., Pastor, K., Putz, Z., Dohnányiová, M., Mat'ašeje, A. and Hampl, R., 'Salivary testosterone levels in preadolescent children', *BMC Pediatrics*, 2(5) (2002).

10 Duke, S., Balzer, B. and Steinbeck, K., 'Testosterone and its effects on human male adolescent mood and behavior: a systematic review', *Journal of Adolescent Health*, 55(3) (September 2014), pp. 315–22.

11 Romans, S., Clarkson, R., Einstein, G., Petrovic, M. and Stewart, D., 'Mood and the menstrual cycle: a review of prospective data studies', *Gender Medicine*, 9(5) (2012), pp. 361–84.

12 Marván, M. L. and Cortés-Iniestra, S., 'Women's beliefs about the prevalence of premenstrual syndrome and biases in recall of premenstrual changes', *Health Psychology*, 20(4) (2001), p. 276.

Chapter 2

1 Maslow, A. H., 'A theory of human motivation', *Psychological Review*, 50(4) (1943), pp. 370–96.

2 Dweck, C. S., *Mindset: The new psychology of success*, Random House (2006).

3 Fleming, N. and Baume, D., 'Learning Styles Again: VARKing up the right tree!', *Educational Developments*, SEDA Ltd, 7.4 (November 2006), pp. 4–7.

Chapter 3

1 Pronin, E. and Olivola, C. Y., 'Egocentrism', in N. J. Salkind., *Encyclopedia of Human Development*, 1 (2006) Thousand Oaks, CA: SAGE Reference, pp. 441–2.

2 Goossens, L., Seiffge-Krenke, I. and Marcoen, A. (1992), 'The many faces of adolescent egocentrism: Two European replications', *Journal of Adolescent Research*, 7(1) (1992), pp. 43–58.

3 Rycek, R. F., Stuhr, S. L., McDermott, J., Benker, J. and Swartz, M. D., 'Adolescent egocentrism and cognitive functioning during late adolescence', *Adolescence*, 33(132) (1998), pp. 745–9.

4   Baron-Cohen, S., Leslie, A. M. and Frith, U., 'Does the autistic child have a "theory of mind"?', *Cognition*, 21(1) (October 1985), pp. 37–46.

5   Milligan, K., Khoury, J., Benoit, D. and Atkinson, L., 'Maternal attachment and mind-mindedness: the role of emotional specificity', *Attachment and Human Development*, 17(3) (2015), pp. 302–18.

6   Peper, J., Koolschijn, P. and Crone, E., 'Development of risk taking: contributions from adolescent testosterone and the orbito-frontal cortex', *Journal of Cognitive Neuroscience*, 25(12) (December 2013), pp. 2141–50.

7   Tymula, A., Rosenberg Belmaker, L., Roy, A., Ruderman, L., Manson, K., Glimcher, P. and Levy, I., 'Adolescents' risk-taking behavior is driven by tolerance to ambiguity', *Proceedings of the National Academy of Sciences of the United States of America*, 109 (42) (2012), pp. 17135–40.

8   Russell, G., Rodgers, L., Ukoumunne, O. and Ford, T., 'Prevalence of Parent-Reported ASD and ADHD in the UK: Findings from the Millennium Cohort Study', *Journal of Autism and Developmental Disorders* (January 2014), pp. 31–40.

9   Aaron, T., Mattfeld, E., Gabrieli, J., Biederman, T., Spencer, A., Brown, A., Kotte, E., Kagan, S. and Whitfield, G., 'Brain differences between persistent and remitted attention deficit hyperactivity disorder', *Brain*, (10) (June 2014).

10 Ellison-Wright, I., Ellison-Wright, Z. and Bullmore, E., 'Structural brain change in Attention Deficit Hyperactivity Disorder identified by meta-analysis', *BMC Psychiatry*, 8: 51 (2008); Kobel, M., Bechtel, N. and Specht, K., 'Structural and functional imaging approaches in attention deficit/hyperactivity disorder: does the temporal lobe play a key role?' *Psychiatry Research*, 83 (2010), pp. 230–36.

11 Baving, L., Laucht M. and Schmidt, M., 'Oppositional children differ from healthy children in frontal brain activation', *Journal of Abnormal Child Psychology*, 28(3) (June 2000), pp. 267–75.

12 Arndt, T., Stodgell, C. and Rodier, P., 'The teratology of autism', *International Journal of Developmental Neuroscience*, 23 (2–3) (2005), pp. 189–99.

13 Geschwind, D., 'Advances in autism', *Annual Review of Medicine*, 60 (2009), pp. 367–80.

14 Schmitz, C. and Rezaie, P., 'The neuropathology of autism: where do we stand?', *Neuropathological Applications in Neurobiology*, 34 (1) (2008), pp. 4–11; Persico, A. and Bourgeron, T., 'Searching for ways out of the autism maze: genetic, epigenetic and

environmental clues', *Trends in Neuroscience*, 29(7) (2006), pp. 349–58.

15 Levy, S., Mandell, D. and Schultz, R., 'Autism', *Lancet*, 374, (9701) (2009), pp. 1627–38.

Chapter 4

1 Gershoff, E. and Grogan-Kaylor, A., 'Spanking and Child Outcomes: Old Controversies and New Meta-Analyses', *Journal of Family Psychology* (7 April 2016), epub ahead of publication at time of writing.

2 Warneke, F. and Tomasello, M., 'Extrinsic rewards undermine altruistic tendencies in 20-month-olds', *Developmental Psychology*, 44(6) (November 2008), pp. 1785–8.

3 Fabes, R. A., Fulse, J., Eisenberg, N., et al., 'Effects of rewards on children's prosocial motivation: A socialization study', *Developmental Psychology*, 25 (1989), pp. 509–15.

4 Kohn, A., *Punished by Rewards: The Trouble with Gold Stars, Incentive Plans, A's, Praise and Other Bribes*, Houghton Mifflin (2000).

5 Brandimonte, M. and Ferrante, D., 'Effects of Material and Non-Material Rewards on Remembering to Do Things for Others', *Frontiers in Human Neuroscience*, 9 (December 2015), p. 647.

6 Cabaj, J., McDonald, S. and Tough, S., 'Early childhood risk and resilience factors for behavioural and emotional problems in middle childhood', *BMC Pediatrics*, 14 (1 July 2014), p. 166.

7 Ahmed, S., Bittencourt-Hewitt, A. and Sebastian, C., 'Neurocognitive bases of emotion regulation development in adolescence', *Developmental Cognitive Neuroscience*, 15 (October 2015), pp. 11–25.

8 Wertz, J., Zavos, H., Matthews, T., Harvey, K., Hunt, A., Pariante, C. and Arseneault, L., 'Why some children with externalising problems develop internalising symptoms: testing two pathways in a genetically sensitive cohort study', *Journal of Child Psychology and Psychiatry*, 56(7) (July 2015), pp. 738–46.

9 Zeiler, M., Waldherr, K., Philipp, J., Nitsch, M., Dür, W., Karwautz, A. and Wagner, G., 'Prevalence of Eating Disorder Risk and Associations with Health-related Quality of Life: Results from a Large School-based Population Screening', *European Eating Disorders Review*, 24(1) (January 2016), pp. 9–18.

10 Grøholt, B., Ekeberg, O. and Haldorsen, T., 'Adolescents

hospitalised with deliberate self-harm: the significance of an intention to die', *European Child Adolescent Psychiatry*, 9(4) (December 2000), pp. 244–54.

11 Ginott, H., *Teacher and Child*, Avon Books (1975).

Chapter 5

1 Holt, J., *How Children Fail*, Penguin Books (1974).

2 Balfanz, R., Byrnes, V. and Fox, J., 'Sent home and put off-track: The antecedents, disproportionalities, and consequences of being suspended in the ninth grade', paper presented at the 'Closing the School Discipline Gap: Research to Practice' conference, Washington, DC (January 2013).

3 Perrya, B. and Morris, E., 'Suspending Progress: Collateral Consequences of Exclusionary Punishment in Public Schools', *American Sociological Review* (5 November 2014).

4 Paksarian, D., Rudolph, K., Jian-Ping, H. and Merikangas, K., 'School Start Time and Adolescent Sleep Patterns: Results From the US National Comorbidity Survey—Adolescent Supplement', *American Journal of Public Health*, 105(7) (July 2015), pp. 1351–7.

Further Reading, Support and Resources

The Gentle Discipline Book on Facebook
    www.facebook.com/GentleDisciplineBook/
Sarah Ockwell-Smith on Facebook
    www.facebook.com/sarahockwellsmithauthor/
Sarah Ockwell-Smith on Twitter
    www.twitter.com/TheBabyExpert
Sarah Ockwell-Smith's website and blog
    www.sarahockwell-smith.com
Sarah Ockwell-Smith's weekly newsletter
    http://bit.ly/1QOiOyF
Gentle Parenting website
    www.gentleparenting.co.uk

Support Organisations

Sensory Processing Foundation
    www.spdfoundation.net/
National Sleep Foundation
    www.sleepfoundation.org
The National Autistic Society
    www.autism.org.uk/

PDA Society
   www.pdasociety.org.uk/
Attention Deficit Disorder Association
   www.add.org/

Books for Children

Books to manage anger

Pudney, W. and Whitehouse, E., *There's a Volcano in my Tummy*, New Society Publishers (1998).

Huebner, D. and Matthews, B., *What to Do When Your Temper Flares*, EDS Publications (2007).

Mundy, M., *Mad Isn't Bad: A Child's Book About Anger*, Abbey Press (2006).

Moses, B. and Gordon, M., *I Feel Angry (Your Emotions)*, Wayland, New edition (1994).

Books for self-esteem

Plummer, D. and Harper, A., *Helping Children to Build Self Esteem*, Jessica Kingsley Publishers (2007).

Sutherland, M., Hancock, N. and Armstrong, N., *Helping Children with Low Esteem: A Guidebook*, Speechmark Publishing (2003).

Sunderland, M. and Armstrong, N., *Ruby and the Rubbish Bin*, Jessica Kingsley Publishers (2007).

Richards, N. and Hague, J., *Being Me and Loving It*, Jessica Kingsley Publishers (2016).

Books about new siblings

Cole, J. and Kightley, R., *I'm a Big Sister*, Harper Festival (2010).

Cole, J. and Kightley, R., *I'm a Big Brother*, Harper Festival (2010).

Communication between mother and daughter

Jacobs, M. and Jacobs, S., *Just Between Us: A No-Stress, No*-Rules *Journal for Girls and Their Moms*, Chronicle Books (2010).

Audio Recordings to Increase Self-esteem

'Relax Kids, Help develop self-esteem and confidence', available on CD from www.relaxkids.com.

Co-operative Game Suggestions

'Race to the Treasure!' by Peaceable Kingdom. Available from Amazon.co.uk and .com.

'Hoot Owl Hoot!', by Peaceable Kingdom. Available from Amazon.co.uk and .com.

'Lost Puppies', by Peaceable Kingdom. Available from Amazon. co.uk and .com.

'Mermaid Island', by Peaceable Kingdom. Available from Amazon.co.uk and .com.

Index

Page numbers in *italics* refer to information contained in tables or illustrations.